A. BIJU KUMAR*, M.Sc., M.Phil., Ph.D., is a Lecturer in the Department of Zoology, N.S.S. College, Ottapalam (Kerala). After completing the M.Sc. course from the Department of Aquatic Biology and Fisheries, University of Kerala, with first rank, he secured M.Phil. and Ph.D. from the same Department. He has undergone an international training course on fish diseases from the Czech Academy of Sciences.*

Dr. Kumar was awarded Kerala University merit scholarship and UGC research fellowship. He is a member of several Fisheries Societies and has published several research papers.

HARISHANKER J. ALAPPAT, *M.Sc., M.Phil., is presently working in Gold Coast Marine Hatchery, Queensland, Australia. After completing M.Sc. and M.Phil. from the Department of Aquatic Biology and Fisheries, University of Kerala, he joined University of Tasmania, Australia, and completed M.Sc. in Aquaculture. He was the recipient of Senior Research Fellowship of CSIR.*

Mr. Alappat is a full member of Asian Fisheries Society and has authored several articles on aquarium fishes.

A COMPLETE GUIDE TO AQUARIUM KEEPING

A COMPLETE GUIDE TO AQUARIUM KEEPING

A. Biju Kumar
and
Harishanker J. Alappat

BOOKS FOR ALL

[A Division of **D.K. Publishers Distributors (P) Ltd.**]
Delhi 110052

Sales Office:
D.K. Publishers Distributors (P) Ltd.
1, Ansari Road, Darya Ganj,
New Delhi-110002.
Phone : 3261465,3278368
Fax : 091-011-3264368

A. Biju Kumar (b. 1968-)
Harishanker J. Alappat (b. 1968-)

ISBN 81-7386-120-X

Published by : **Books For All**
[A Division of D.K. Publishers Distributors (P) Ltd.]
Regd. Office : A-6, Nimri Community Centre,
Near Bharat Nagar, Ashok Vihar, Phase-IV, Delhi 110052.
Phone : 7430113, 7143353

Laser Typesetting by : **DataGraph Systems,** Delhi 110052.

Printed at : **D.K. Fine Art Press (P) Ltd.**, Delhi-110052.

PRINTED IN INDIA

PREFACE

Aquarium keeping, which began centuries ago in China and Rome, has now grown into one of the most popular hobbies of the modern world. In addition, ornamental fish trade is a flourishing business in Asian countries. India has its own stock of over 100 species of freshwater ornamental fishes. Ornamental fish culture and export is yet to pick up momentum in India. A comprehensive book dealing with various aspects of aquarium keeping is lacking in India. This publication is brought out in order to meet the demand of hobbyists and culturists interested in fish keeping and ornamental fish culture. We hope that this publication would also serve the needs of students interested in fisheries and aquaculture. It is needless to say that it is impossible for us to include the varieties of freshwater aquarium fishes in this book. However, we have tried to include representatives from all the major families of aquarium fishes. In addition, aquarium management, breeding and diseases of ornamental fishes have been given special emphasis. Some Indian ornamental fishes like Banded loach, Indian stone sucker, Sand loach and Malabar baril which have hitherto found no place in aquariums have also been included.

We are grateful to Sri. K.G. Padmanabhan, former curator, Aquarium, Trivandrum, Prof. C.M. Aravindan and Dr. S. Radhakrishnan, Department of Aquatic Biology and Fisheries, University of Kerala, Trivandrum, for critical suggestions for improving the quality of this book. Thanks are due to Mrs. Lakshmi Sasidharan and Mr. V. Shibuvardhanan for sketching some of the figures for the text. We are thankful to Miss Anuradha Rammohan for her assistance in various stages of preparation of this book.

Since this is a pioneering attempt of this type in India, we welcome suggestions from readers and well-wishers.

A. Biju Kumar
Harishanker J. Alappat

CONTENTS

		Page No.
Preface		vii
List of Figures		xiii
1.	**INTRODUCTION**	**1**
2.	**HISTORY OF FISH KEEPING**	**2**
3.	**AQUARIUM MANAGEMENT**	**3**
	Tank	3
	Lighting	4
	Temperature	4
	Water	4
	Layout of the Aquarium	5
	Filtration	5
	Aeration	7
	Aquarium Plants	7
	Selection and Introduction of Fish	12
	Feeding	13
	Maintenance of Aquarium	18
4.	**COMMON AQUARIUM FISHES**	**21**
	Egg Layers	**21**
	Knife Fish	21
	Cardinal Tetra	21
	Black Widow Tetra	22
	Buenos Aires Tetra	23
	Serpae Tetra	23
	Red Eye Tetra	24
	Neon Tetra	24

Hockey Stick Tesas 25
Striped Head Stander 26
Piŕanha 26
Hatchet Fish 28
Malabar Baril 28
Zebra Danio 29
Leopard Danio 29
Giant Danio 29
Flying Barb 30
Long fin Barb 31
Rosy Barb 31
Black Spot Barb 32
Melon Barb 33
Tiger Barb 33
Slender Rasbora 34
Gold Fish 35
Koi Carp 36
Sand Loach 37
Banded Loach 38
Coolie Loach 38
'Y' Loach 39
Indian Glass Catfish 39
Dwarf Catfishes 40
Indian Glass Fish 41
Leopard Scat 41
Oscar Cichlid 42
Firemouth Cichlid 43
Orange Chromide 44

	Pearl Spot	44
	Angel Fish	45
	Discus	47
	Siamese Fighting Fish	48
	Dwarf Gourami	49
	Paradise Fish	50
	Pearl Gourami	50
	Blue Gourami	51
	Kissing Gourami	52
	Live bearing fishes	**52**
	Guppy	53
	Mollies	54
	Sword Tail	55
	Platy	57
5.	**BREEDING**	**59**
6.	**DISEASES**	**65**
	Glossary	77

List of Figures

		Page
1.	Biological Filter	6
2.	*Ambulia*	7
3.	Madagascar Lace-Leaf Plant	8
4.	Madagascar Sword Plant	8
5.	Indian Fern	9
6.	*Cryptocoryne beckettii*	9
7.	*C. ciliata*	9
8.	*C. cordata*	9
9.	Amazon Sword Plant	10
10.	Arrowhead	10
11.	Eel Grass (spiral)	10
12.	Duck Weed	11
13.	*Pistia*	11
14.	Crystalwort	11
15.	*Salvinia*	11
16.	Brine Shrimp	14
17.	Blood Worm	14
18.	Water Flea	15
19.	*Moina*	15
20.	*Moinadaphnia*	15
21.	Rotifer (*Brachionus*)	16
22.	Mosquito Larvae	16
22a.	Set-up of the Home Aquarium	19
23.	Knife Fish	21
24.	Cardinal Tetra	22
25.	Black Widow Tetra	22
26.	Buenos Aires Tetra	23
27.	Serpae Tetra	24
28.	Neon Tetra	25
29.	Hockey Stick Tesas	25
30.	Striped Head Stander	26
31.	Piranha	27
32.	Hatchet Fish	28
33.	Malabar Baril	28
34.	Zebra Danio	29

35.	Giant Danio	30
36.	Flying Barb	30
37.	Long Fin Barb	31
38.	Rosy Barb	32
39.	Black Spot Barb	32
40.	Melon Barb	33
41.	Tiger Barb	34
42.	Slender Rasbora	35
43.	Gold Fish	36
44.	Koi Carp	37
45.	Sand Loach	37
46.	Banded Loach	38
47.	Coolie Loach	38
48.	'Y' Loach	39
49.	Indian Glass Catfish	39
50.	Corydora Catfish	40
51.	Indian Glass Fish	41
52.	Leopard Scat	42
53.	Oscar Cichlid	43
54.	Firemouth Cichlid	43
55.	Orange Chromide	44
56.	Pearl Spot	45
57.	Angel Fish	46
58.	Discus	47
59.	Siamese Fighting Fish	48
60.	Dwarf Gourami	49
61.	Paradise Fish	50
62.	Pearl Gourami	51
63.	Blue/Three spot Gourami	51
64.	Kissing Gourami	52
65.	Guppy	53
66.	Tail Patterns of Guppy	53
67.	Sail Fin Molly	54
68.	Black Molly	55
69.	Sword Tail	55
70.	Sex Reversal in Sword Tail (Female to Male)	56
71a.	Wagtail Platy	57
71b.	Simpson Platy	58
71c.	Spitz Platy	58
71d.	Variegated Platy	58

72.	Conditioning of Fish for Breeding	60
73.	Spawning Grid	61
74-76.	Different Breeding Techniques to Separate Eggs/Young Ones from Parents	62-64
77.	*Ichthyophthirius multifilis*	67
78.	*Myxobolus sp.*	68
79.	*Trichodina*	68
80.	*Oodinium*	69
81.	Anchor Worm	69
82.	Ergasilus	69
83.	Fish Leech	70
84.	Fish Lice	70
85.	Gill Flukes	71
86.	Sucking Worm	71
87.	Tape Worm	71
88.	Spiny-Headed Worm	72
89.	Round Worm	72
90.	Common Diseases of Aquarium Fish	75

INTRODUCTION

Fishes are no doubt one of the most beautiful and lovable of all pets. Watching those splendorously coloured fishes flittering about in the aquarium takes one to the world of joy and excitement and helps one forget the worries and tensions of the fast paced modern day life.

Rearing fish in an aquarium means providing ideal living conditions for the fish, very similar to that in nature. Today, fish keeping has grown into one of the most popular hobbies in all parts of the world. Aquarium has a pivotal position in all modern interior decorations.

Of nearly 20,000 fish species available in the world, only very small percentage is represented by ornamental fishes. Ornamental fishes are gaining importance mainly because of their high demand and tremendous export potential. At present, the total turnover from aquarium trade already exceeds 4,000 million US dollars. Lion's share of this trade is contributed by Asian countries, which comes to nearly 70% of the total. Nearly 85% of the ornamental fish trade is represented by freshwater ornamental fishes.

The demand for tropical ornamental fishes far exceeds their availability or supply. Initially ornamental fishes were collected from natural water bodies. However, availability of ornamental fish is fast reaching its limits due to over exploitation and pollution of natural water bodies. To satisfy the growing demand for ornamental fishes, intensive breeding programmes have been practiced these days.

Majority of Indian ornamental fish breeders concentrate on certain very common varieties. Hence the demand for rare ornamental fishes is very high. India has its own stock of over 100 species of freshwater ornamental fishes. *Puntius melanampyx* (melon barb), *Colisa chuna* (Honey gourami), *Danio malabaricus* (Giant danio), *Botia dario* (Necktie loach), *B. geto, B. almorhae* (Striped or Tiger loach) and catfishes *(Gagata* and *Nangra)* are the Indian fishes which are quite new additions to aquariums. Since these fishes are new and rare, they have high demand in the international market.

In this book we are including some Indian fishes which have hitherto found no place in aquariums anywhere in the world. These compatible and companiable fishes like Barilius *backeri* (Malabar Baril), *Lepidocephalus thermalis* (sand Loach) and *Noemacheilus triangularis* (Banded Loach) have been found to do well in aquariums.

HISTORY OF FISH KEEPING

Ever since the beginning of human civilisation man kept animals and birds as a source of food or to help him in hunting. However, he realised the importance of fish only in the later stages of human civilisation. When we look back at the history we can see that the fish culture began in China as early as 1000 B.C. They started fish culture with common carp, *Cyprinus carpio*. Keeping fishes as pets was started by Romans. By the end of the second century B.C. fish keeping had become a fashion in Rome.

Domestication of gold fishes began on a large scale in China during the Sung Dynasty (960-1278). From China gold fishes were transported to different parts of the world. Chinese kept these gold fishes in small containers, which were probably the world's first aquaria. However, Romans were the first to keep fishes in glass aquaria. During 18th century, Hungarians kept loaches as 'weather fishes' to forecast storms (when the atmospheric pressure falls, the loaches get agitated and come frequently to the water surface to gulp atmospheric air). The first tropical fish to be kept in home aquarium is supposed to be the Paradise fish, *Macropodus opercularis*.

Early in the 18th century gold fishes were transported to England from China and kept in small glass bowls. This became a popular hobby in England which is still practised throughout the world. From England gold fishes were transported to different parts of the world by the end of the 18th century. This increased interest for aquarium keeping paved way for the establishment of the world's first public aquarium in London during 1853 — "the fish house" in Regent's park Zoo. The first marine aquarium was started at Paris in 1860. The Berlin aquarium opened in 1869 used artificial seawater for the first time. German ichthyologists collected various varieties of ornamental fishes from different parts of the world and began a large scale ornamental fish trade. A large number of aquaria were set up in different parts of the world during 19th and 20th centuries. As the availability of ornamental fishes from natural water bodies started declining, people began to think about rearing them in captivity. Today, most of the aquarium fishes are bred in captivity on a large scale to meet the higher demand.

AQUARIUM MANAGEMENT

Proper scientific and practical knowledge is necessary to select tank, plants and fishes for an aquarium. One should try to simulate natural conditions in an aquarium. For successful fish keeping, different water conditions like temperature, oxygen, hardness, pH (hydrogen ion concentration) and other factors like lighting, feeding, planting,etc. should be taken into account. An aquarist should have the basic idea about the biology of fishes and different factors controlling their growth in the aquarium tank.

3.1.Tank

The fish tank is the basic equipment for all home aquaria. Though tanks are available in various shapes and sizes, the most popular one is the metal framed rectangular tank. Frameless glass tanks are suitable for marine aquaria. Moulded tanks look attractive but many of them have visual distortions. Moreover, if damaged, repairing is a tedious job. A simple angle-iron (metal) tank is both strong and durable. Different types of commonly available aquarium tanks and their capacities are given in Table I. Beginners are advised to start with double cube tank (60 x 30 x 30 cm). It is always better to use large tanks since it is easier to keep a larger tank in good condition.

Table I : Common Tank Sizes and Their Capacities

Length (cm)	*Width (cm)*	*Depth (cm)*	*Surface area (cm^2)*	*Volume (Litres)*	*Weight of water (kg)*	*Maximum Fish Capacity (cm)*
30	15	15	450	8	8	15
45	25	25	1,125	35	35	38
60	30	30	1,800	67	67	60
90	30	30	2,700	101	101	90
120	30	30	3,600	135	135	120

Since water is very heavy, it is essential to have a strong supporting stand. Tanks can be kept in a table, similar furniture or in an iron stand specially made for the purpose. The tank should be placed at a firm and level site.

If you are not satisfied with the commonly available tanks at the shop, you can make your own tank. The glasses used should be optically clear and be of sufficient thickness to withstand the pressure of water. The glass plates can be joined by aquarium cements, silicon glue (silicon rubber sealant), etc. You can also make built-in aquarium in your home by installing a glass plate in the front part of the concrete tank.

It is better to keep the tank away from direct sunlight to avoid over heating and excessive algal growth. Instead of the window sill, a place near the window sill, preferably getting northern light may be selected. It is advisable to decorate the tanks after placing it to its permanent position. Small leaks may occur in some tanks initially which may be sealed automatically after some time. If leaks continue for long time, it can be sealed with silicon rubber sealant, battery compound, etc. Care should be taken not to move the tank with water as this may lead to severe leakage.

3.2. Lighting

Keeping the aquarium tanks away from direct sunlight and illuminating it with artificial light is more safe and makes the tank more attractive. Excessive exposure to sunlight may result in algal blooms.

Lights can be mounted in the aquarium cover —the hood or reflector. Lamps installed at the front part of the reflector is more ideal as it produces shadows away from the viewer. Though the amount of light required in an aquarium is a matter of experience, according to Mills (1984) a 30 cm long aquarium tank requires 40 watts (tungsten lamp) or 10 watts (fluorescent lamp) light. Fluorescent lighting was found to be more successful and economical. The illuminating sources should not touch the water or the glass.

3.3. Temperature

Most of the tropical fishes prefer temperature between 22 and 25°C. However even in some regions of tropical countries, it is not possible to get uniform temperature in all seasons. These temperature changes in aquarium water can be measured by means of thermometers — mercury or alcohol. Thermometers, either floating or adhesive type, should be kept in the place where it can be easily read. It should be kept away from the heater or the light source since in such cases it affects the thermometer reading. Heaters and thermostats are used for maintaining optimum temperature in the aquarium. 125 watts heater would be sufficient for a double cube tank. Heaters should be installed in the lower part of the aquarium tank for maximum efficiency and be immersed in water before operation. Thermostat is a device which automatically switches off when the desired temperature is achieved. Generally, the thermostat is kept at the range 20-25°C.

3.4. Water

Good quality water is, no doubt, the most important component of the aquarium. Any type of the pure natural water can be used for keeping aquarium fishes. Tap water for domestic purposes is usually disinfected by Chlorine which is harmful to fish. The effect of Chlorine can be neutralised by exposure to sunlight and to strong aeration for 2 to 3 days or by adding hyposolution (Sodium thiosulphate). While selecting water for the aquarium, hardness and pH (hydrogen ion concentration) should be given prior consideration. Beginners may not worry too much about these factors. These factors will come to the forefront only while breeding aquarium fishes.

Hardness of water is mainly due to dissolved salts, particularly calcium and magnesium. Hardness is usually measured in parts per million (ppm). Water with a hardness less than 100 ppm is called soft water and greater than 200 ppm is called hard water. Hardness of water can be reduced by diluting with distilled water and increased by adding chalk or lime stone. The optimum hardness of water required for aquarium fishes vary in different species.

pH or hydrogen ion concentration is a measure of relative acidity and alkalinity of water. Neutral water has a pH of 7, while water with a pH less than 7 is acidic and greater than 7 is alkaline. Regarding pH also each species of fish has its own preference. Test kits are now available in market to measure hardness and pH of water.

3.5. Layout of the Aquarium

Aquarium floor may be furnished with sand, gravel, mosaic chips, pebbles, rocks,etc., sloping gradually from a depth of 6 to 10 cm at the back wall to 5 cm or less in the front. Light coloured and medium sized (2 to 3 mm) gravel has been found to be good for this purpose. However, certain types of rocks which distintegrate in water (eg. lime stone) should be avoided. All these materials should be washed thoroughly before use to prevent clouding of water. Nowadays, laminated or water proof posters of various aquarium flora are stuck to the back pane of the aquarium to provide background scenery to the indoor aquarium. Other decoratives like drift wood, roots, synthetic decoratives, etc. could be used according to one's choice to provide pleasant background for the aquarium.

3.6. Filtration

The water of a living aquarium is likely to get polluted by waste products from different sources like excretory products of fish, dead plants and animals, uneaten food,etc. Disintegration of these waste material release large amount of ammonia, the concentration of which beyond 0.5 mg/1 is toxic to fish. Hence it is necessary to convert highly toxic ammonia to nitrite and then to nitrate which is non toxic and may be absorbed by plants as their nutrients.

Different types of filters — both internal and external — are available in aquarium shops to clear aquarium water. The siphon inlet tube should be submerged in water and the filters should be filled with water by siphon action before operation.

Unlike the box type filters, biological filters rely on bacteria (hence the name biological filter) to break down toxic ammonia to nitrite and nitrates. Biological filter or under gravel filter comprises a corrugated and porous asbestos or plastic plate. This plate is kept slightly above the bottom with the help of suction pads, non soluble and non toxic glues etc. In cases where anchoring devices are absent, these sheets show a tendency to float up which can be prevented by keeping few pebbles over it. A cylindrical tube of 8 cm diameter opened at both the ends, is inserted into an opening made at one end of the plate as shown in the Fig. 1. Such plates could be purchased from aquarium shops. After installing the plate, cover it with a layer of gravel atleast 5 cm deep. In order to give a better appearance, slope the gravel from back to the front of the tank. Large pebbles should be avoided since they can trap food particles and waste materials between them. Further, they allow speedy flow of water through the filter which makes the biological filtration ineffective. The biological filter is operated by air from the air pump.

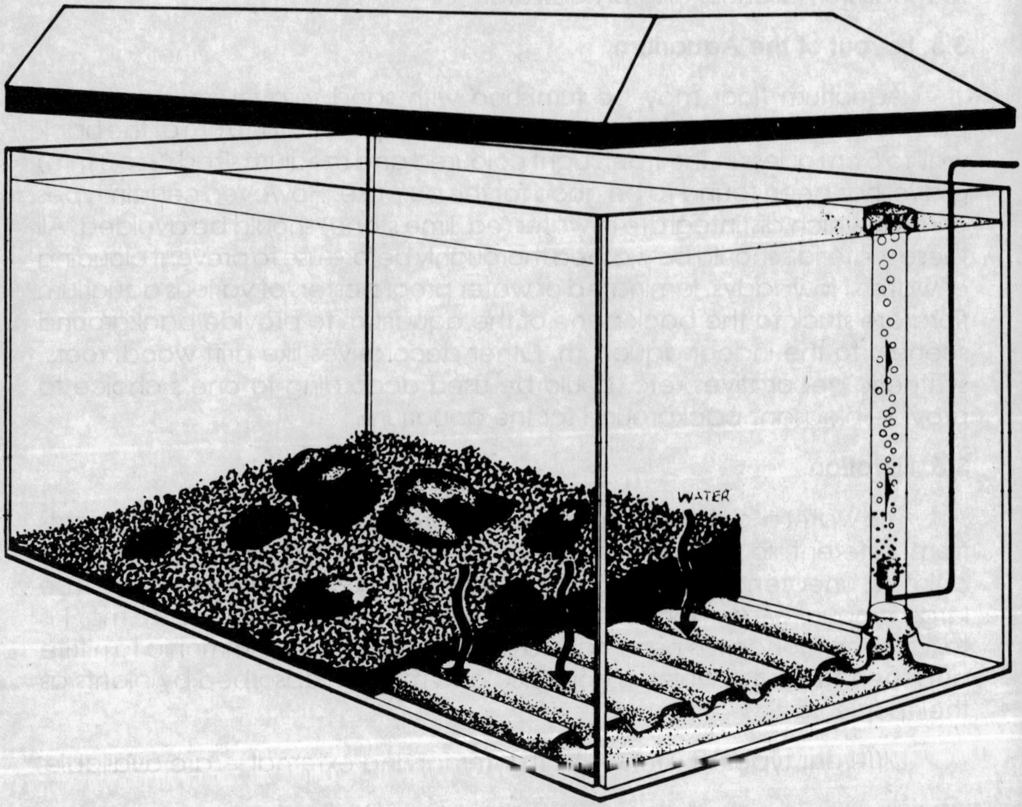

Fig. 1

A colony of bacteria develops in the gravel bed as the aquarium water passes through it slowly. The toxic ammonia present in the aquarium water is converted into non poisonous nitrate by bacteria present in the gravel bed. The nitrate rich water thus occupying the lowest region of the tank is brought to the surface with the help of air pump. Thus the same water is used again and again. Care should be taken not to switch off biological filter for long time, since it may affect the growth of bacterial colony present in it. In aquaria where filtration unit has not been installed, partial water exchange in every two weeks and periodical removal of wastes are recommended.

3.7. Aeration

Aeration is necessary in aquarium, particularly during night hours when the carbon dioxide level goes up due to respiration of plants and fish. The air bubbles produced by aerators create ripples on the water surface which facilitates easy oxygen exchange between atmospheric air and the water and drives out carbon dioxide from water. Various types of aerators, both piston type and vibratory type, are available from aquarium shops ; the latter being most common and less expensive.

3.8. Aquarium Plants

Besides producing oxygen through the process of photosynthesis, plants act as 'purifiers' and 'beautifiers' in an aquarium. They provide food, shade, shelter and spawning ground for several fishes. Further, aquarium plants inhibit the unnecessary growth of algae in the aquarium. Different forms of aquarium plants are described below.

3.8.1. Rooted Plants

Fig. 2

1. *Ambulia* (*Limnophila*) (Fig. 2) : This Indian plant closely resembling *Cabomba*, grows faster and easily multiplies from stem cuttings. This plant has a light green shade which gives a pleasant background for the aquarium.

2. *Ditch Moss* (*Anacharis or Elodea*) : Ditch moss is probably the fastest growing and the best oxygenator among aquarium plants. Further, some aquarists claim that it cleans green water. These plants are more suitable for outdoor ponds.

3. The Madagascar Plant (*Aponogeton spp.*) : *Aponogeton* represents one of the magnificent plants of the home aquarium. They can be cultivated in small flower pots with coarse sand.

The Madagascar Lace-leaf Plant (*A. fenestralis*) (Fig. 3) and the Madagascar sword plant (*A. undulatus*) (Fig. 4) are the important varieties. They reproduce from their bulb (rhizome).

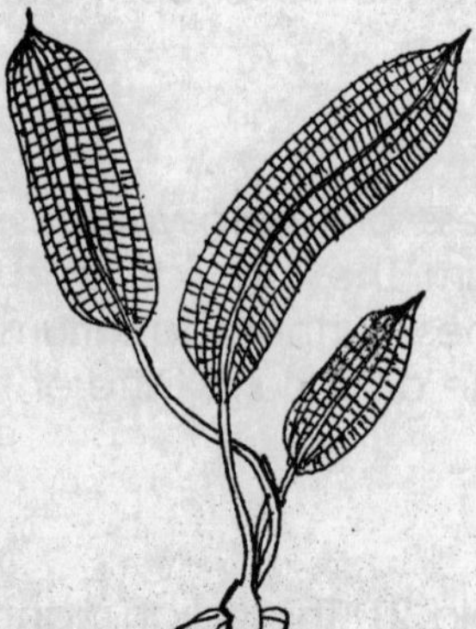

Fig. 3

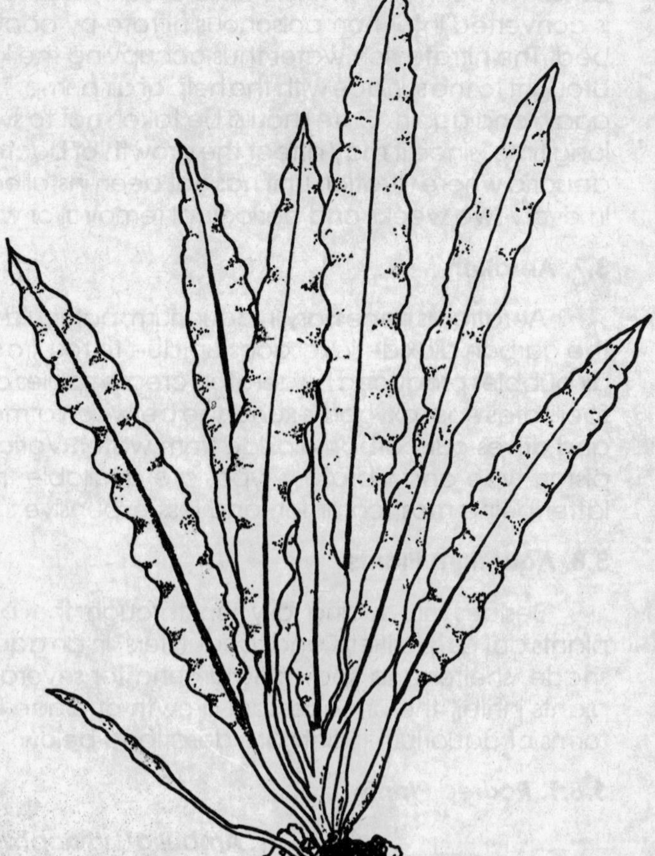

Fig. 4

Fragile leaves and a rest period during December-January (when the plant dies down) are the faults of this plant.

4. Fanwort or Water Shield (*Cabomba*) : Fanwort is widely grown and its fanнshaped light green leaves on a rúnning stem form an excellent spawning medium for fishes. They need strong sunlight and clean water for proper growth. It can be easily reared from stem cuttings.

5. *Hornwort* (*Ceratophyllum*): This plant growing abundantly in strong sunlight is a good oxygenator and makes a fine floating shelter for adult fishes and refuge for young fishes. However,this plant is brittle and has no roots, hence suitable only for outdoor spawning tanks.

Fig. 5

6. *Indian Fern or Water Sprite* (*Ceratopteris thalictorides* (Fig. 5) : This plant can be grown either rooted or floating. This fast growing plant that thrives well in strong sunlight reproduce either from stem cuttings or from daughter plants formed from the surface of the leaves. Aged parent plant should be trimmed and replaced periodically.

7. *Cryptocoryne spp.* : These Asiatic plants with thick dark green leaves have the advantage of growing healthy for a long time in situations where sunlight is rather scarce. They are good foreground plants i.e., they can be planted in the anterior part of the aquarium tank. They can be cultivated in small flower pots with sand and earth. They propagate mainly from runners. Important Cryptocorynes are *C. beckettii* (Fig. 6), *C. ciliata* (Fig. 7), *C. cordata* (Fig. 8), etc.

Fig. 6

Fig. 7

Fig. 8

8. *The Amazon Sword Plant* (*Echinodorus* spp.) (Fig. 9): *Echinodorus* is the most popular specimen plant cultivated usually in small flower pots, embedded in the aquarium gravel. This short stemmed plant having abundantly growing leaves, grows well even under conditions of artificial illumination. It reproduces small plants from the runners.

9. *Hair Grass* (*Eleocharis*) : This variety item with needle like leaves requires good sunlight for proper growth. It makes an excellent spawning grass, both for live-bearers and for egg layers. Majority of hair grasses propagate by means of runners.

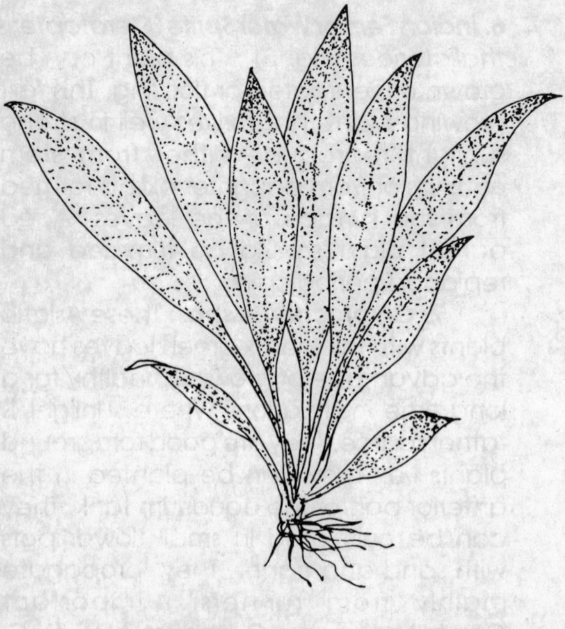

Fig. 9

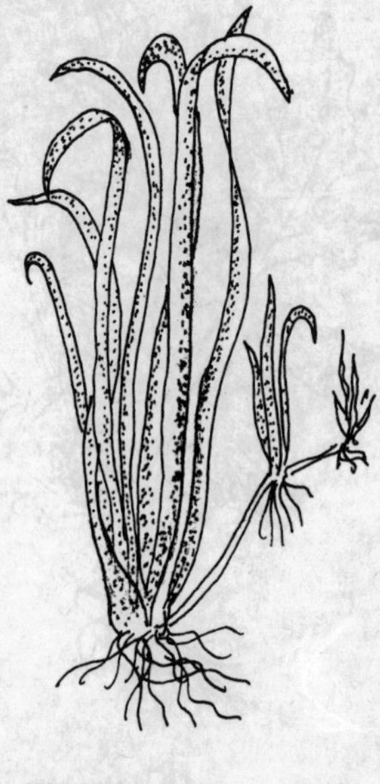

Fig. 10

10. *Arrowhead* (Fig. 10) (*Sagittaria*) : Arrowhead is a popular grass-like aquatic plant that has tough, arrow shaped areal leaves, hence the name. They are good oxygenators and since their roots are fast growing they should be planted in sand of about 5 cm deep. *Sagittaria* reproduce by means of runners and grow fast in the presence of strong sunlight.

11. *Eel Grass or Tape Grass* (*Vallisneria*): This beautiful grass-like background plant has narrow, light green leaves which grows vertically, spreading its leaves at the top layer of aquarium water. This plant is one of the best oxygenators and its roots tend to purify the soil. There are separate male and female plants. *Vallisneria* propagate by means of runners. *V. spiralis* (Corkscrew Vallisneria) (Fig. 11) and *V. torta* (Common Eel Grass) are the most common varieties.

As *Sagittaria* and *Vallisneria* often compete with each other, both are seldom planted together in the aquarium.

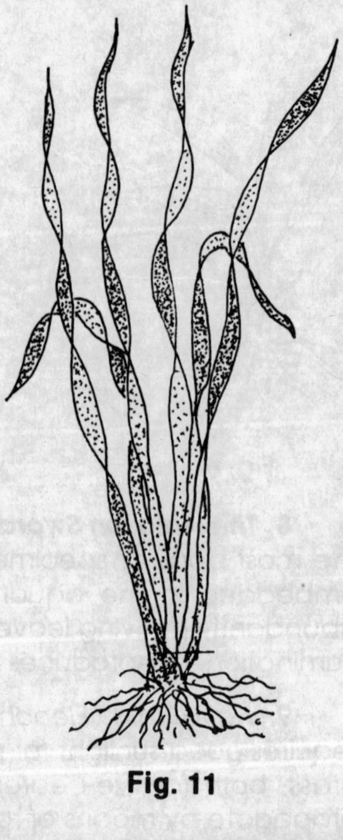

Fig. 11

3.8.2. Floating Plants

1. *Duckweed* (*Lemna minor*) (Fig. 12) : In addition to providing shade, duckweed form food to some of the aquarium fishes like goldfish. Further, dried duckweed is used for producing infusoria.

2. *Pistia* (Fig. 13) : It is a beautiful floating plant with velvety green leaves and long roots. They propagate by means of runners. The long brushy roots give shelter to young fish.

3. *Crystalwort* (*Riccia*) (Fig. 14) : Best suited for outdoor breeding plants, *Riccia* grows well under strong light. It is an ideal plant for shading the aquarium and for holding the spawn in the case of bubble nest builders. In addition, they act as good oxygenators. Some aquarium fishes like Leopard scat consumes them as their main food.

4. *Salvinia*: (Fig. 15): These plants with large velvety green leaves multiply quickly in warm, moist atmosphere. Their trailing roots provide shelter for baby fishes.

Fig. 12

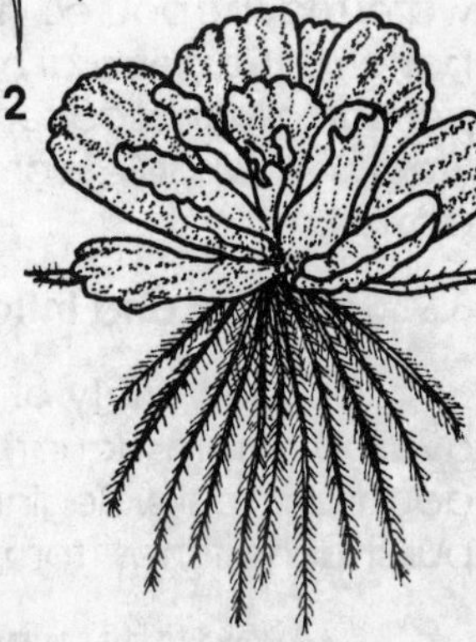

Fig. 13

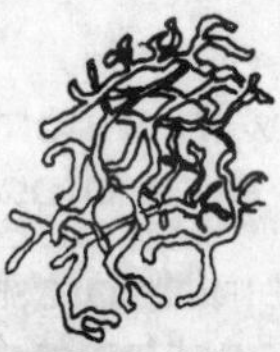

Fig. 14

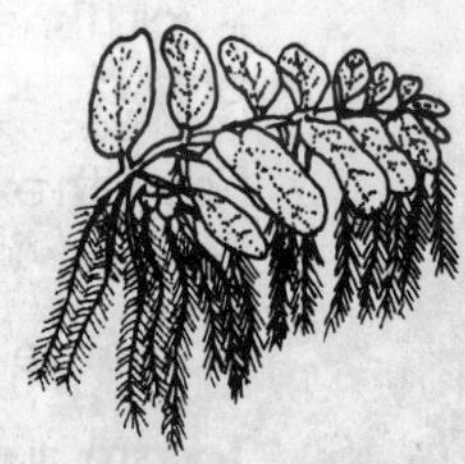

Fig. 15

3.8.3. Planting

Aquarium tank should be filled 1/3rd with water before planting in order to avoid overflowing and clouding. Before planting, the plants should be thoroughly washed to remove dirt,pathogens and other unwanted organisms attached to it. If needed, plants may be disinfected by rinsing with 0.1 % Potassium alum solution followed by washing in tap water. Plants must be kept moist before planting (preferably between wet news papers) to prevent them from drying. Coarse sand or a mixture of sand and pebbles are found to be suitable for planting.

The gravel or sand in the aquarium tank should be deep enough to hold the rooted plants. Roots of large plants should be kept completely under the sand to prevent them from floating. For some large plants like arrowhead and eel grass , the gravel should be atleast 5 cm deep. Rocks and other decoratives, if any, should be installed before planting. If large quantity of water is present in the tank, plants may be installed using a forked wooden piece or planting sticks. Planting large plants in deeper sand in the back and sides of the tank, smaller plants in the middle and bushy plants in the corners and between rocks will enhance the beauty of the aquarium. Large plants like the Amazon sword plant could be planted in small flower pots.

Water filling could be continued after planting and the water level should be kept around 5 cm below the top of the tank. While filing the aquarium tank, care should be taken to prevent the water from disturbing the bottom. For that, water may be poured into a piece of paper or polythene sheet kept above the bottom. The general held belief that aquarium water should be removed periodically is not correct. However, partial water change in every two to three weeks is advisable in order to maintain the equilibrium of oxygen and carbon dioxide.

3.9. Selection and Introduction of Fish

A wide variety of exotic and indigenous ornamental fish species are available from aquarium shops and natural water bodies for stocking in aquarium tanks. Beginners should keep the following points in mind before purchasing fishes from shops.

1. Avoid fishes which show signs of sluggishness or abnormal swimming behaviour.
2. Avoid fishes with abnormal body parts like distended belly, protruding and cloudy eyes, dropping fins etc.
3. Fish with external parasites, nodules, haemorrhages, wounds, fungus-like growth and frayed fins should not be selected.
4. Do not select fish which are reluctant to accept food.
5. Too small and too large fishes should be avoided when selecting fish for the community tank.
6. Beginners are advised not to start with expensive fishes. First make sure that you can rear the fishes successfully by beginning with smaller and less expensive fishes like the live bearers.

Before introducing fishes into the aquarium tank, it is better to keep them in a separate quarantine tank for a few days. This is usually done to observe the fish for the occurrence of diseases, if any. If symptoms of disease occur, they may be treated with 2 % Potassium permanganate solution. Prior to releasing the fishes into the quarantine tank, the polythene bag or container containing the fishes should be kept floating in the quarantine tank in order to acclimatise the fishes to the temperature of the tank. The same should be done while transferring fishes from the quarantine tank to the aquarium tank, if the conditions of both the tanks differ drastically. Another method of acclimatising fish is by adding aquarium water little by little into the container containing fish and finally filling the entire container with aquarium water. It is better to introduce the fish two to three days after planting, since by that time the water will become clear and well oxygenated.

Before stocking one should have an idea about the number of fishes that could be stocked in an aquarium tank (holding capacity). The holding capacity of the tank depends mainly on the surface area of the tank, its oxygen content and size of the fish (see Table 1). There is no definite calculation to show the exact number of fishes that could be stocked in an aquarium. However, according to Mills (1989) it is practical to allow 75 cm^2 water for every 2.5 cm of fish body length (standard length). For example, an aquarium tank with a water surface area of 2700 cm^2 will support a total of 90 cm fish i.e., 10 fishes of 9 cm length or 15 fishes of 6 cm length. But this type of calculation has been found to be useful only for tropical freshwater fishes.

Different species of fish are stocked together in a community tank. Avoid stocking fish which chase, attack or prey upon other members of the community tank. Different fish species occupy different areas (niches) in an aquarium. For example, Danios and Guppies occupy upper column of water, Angel fish, Platies and Sword tails occupy the middle column and loaches occupy the lower column. By stocking fishes which occupy different areas, one can exploit all the areas available in the aquarium, thus avoiding competition for food and space.

3.10 Feeding

Tropical aquarium fish feed fall into two categories. 1. live or natural and 2. prepared or artificial. It is difficult to say which type is suitable for fishes because some fishes respond well to the natural food and some to artificial. It is practicable not to stick on to a particular food for a long time. The rate of feeding in fishes have been found to increase with increase in temperature and oxygen content. It is better to feed the fishes twice a day, early in the morning and in the evening. In the colder months or winter it is advisable to feed the fish only once every day. The quantity of food given at a particular time should be limited to that which can be consumed within five minutes. Both overfeeding and underfeeding are equally harmful. Excess and unused food in the aquarium pollutes the water very quickly and should be removed immediately. Hence beginners are advised to stick on to slight underfeeding than overfeeding. Based on feeding habits, fishes can be classified into herbivores (feeding on plant matter), carnivores (feeding on animal matter) and omnivores (feeding on both plant and animal matter).

Feeding rings may be used for confining feeds within a small area, thus avoiding the spread of food all over the water. In addition it teaches the fish to expect food at a particular place. Floating feeding rings are mainly used to feed tubifex worms. As the worms escape very slowly through the holes of the feeding rings, fish can feed them at their leisure. Fish can be trained to accept food from the hands of their owner by supplying food after making ripples in the water using your fingers. After few days of training the fish will come to you as soon as your fingers make contact with the water.

3.10.1. Live food

1. Brine Shrimp or Artemia (Fig. 16): The brine shrimp, *Artemia* is a crustacean resembling shrimp, commonly found in hyper saline waters. Brine shrimp is perhaps the most popular of all the live food used in aquaria. They have very high protein content (40 to 60 %) and is totally free from pathogens. The eggs of brine shrimp can be stored dry indefinitely. The eggs are not used directly as food. The newly hatched larvae (nauplius larva) are used as food for young fishes. Two types of brine shrimp eggs are available in the market, capsulated (shelled) and non capsulated; the latter is supposed to be better.

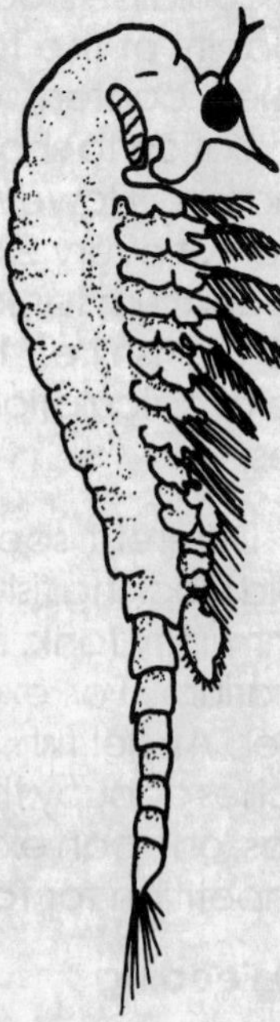

Fig. 16

Brine shrimp eggs can be purchased from aquarium shops and fish feed manufacturers. The eggs can be hatched out by placing it in a glass jar containing sea water (or add two teaspoons full of common salt to one litre of tap water) for 20 to 24 hours with continuous aeration. The hatching time may be increased by increasing the salinity. Aeration is stopped for 10 to 15 minutes after incubation to allow the egg capsules to float. Then cover the upper part of the jar with a black cloth. The nauplii collected at the bottom of the jar can be drained out easily. These larvae can be directly fed to the young fishes. Baby shrimps make an excellent food for young fishes. In addition frozen larval and adult forms of brine shrimp have been used as food for aquarium fishes.

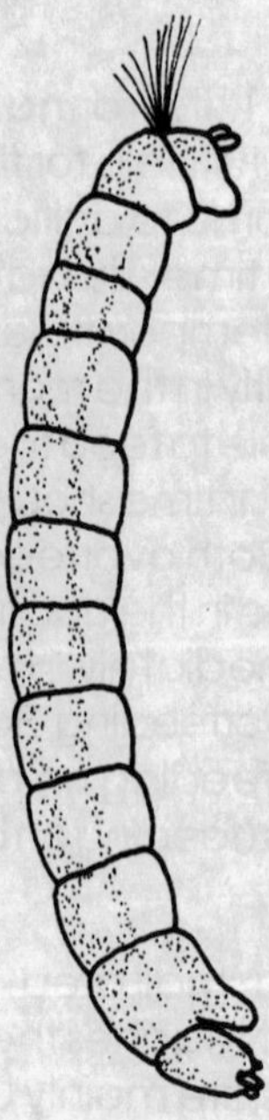

Fig. 17

2. Blood Worms (Fig. 17): These are not true worms, but are the larvae of *Chironomous* midges. They are bright red in colour and are common in ponds and other natural water bodies with decaying organic matter. Blood worms (size 1 - 1.5 cm) are excellent food for larger fishes. Do not use blood worms in tanks containing small fry since they are capable of killing small fishes.

Unused agriculture fields, shallow ponds or concrete tanks with muddy bottom could be used for culturing blood worms. As the first step, culture system is cleaned and dried to remove all the unwanted organisms. Then these ponds are fertilised with organic manures (piggery manure, cattle manure,etc.) and inorganic fertilizers (Urea, superphosphate,etc.). After fertilization, the ponds are filled with water (nearly 15 cm). Chironomid adults now start laying eggs in the culture system. The larvae hatched out from the eggs reach cultivable size in one month which can be collected using nylon nets.

3. Water Flea (*Daphnia*) (Fig. 18): Water flea is one of the popular live foods preferred by all fishes, particularly young ones. Water flea is a small free floating cladoceran (Arthropoda) often bright red in colour, commonly found in stagnant freshwater bodies through out the world. They can be collected from ponds using a fine nylon net, preferably at dawn. If available in large numbers, they can be kept frozen in the refrigerator for a few days without losing its nutritional value.

In order to maintain a ready and steady supply of water flea particularly in breeding ponds, they can be artificially cultured in large quantities. Fibre glass, plastic or concrete tanks of 100 to 2000 litre capacity have been used for culturing water flea. It can also be cultured in outdoor ponds of nearly 60 cm depth receiving good amount of sunlight. The culture system is then filled with Chlorine free water and fertilised with organic and inorganic fertilizers and groundnut oil cake. Water flea collected from natural water bodies can be introduced into the culture system at the rate of 1-2 Nos./ml of water as the water in the culture system turns green after fertilization. Water flea multiplies rapidly and can be collected in vast numbers within a week using nylon nets.

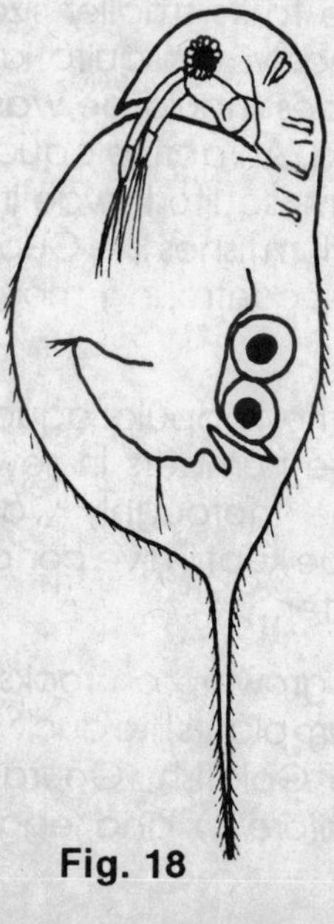

Fig. 18

Fig. 19

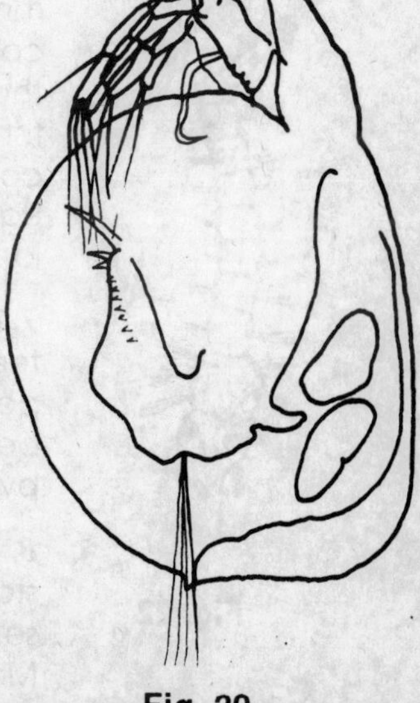

Fig. 20

Other cladocerans similar to Daphnia like *Moina* (Fig. 19) and *Moinadaphnia* (Fig. 20), common in the freshwater systems of India have been observed as excellent food of aquarium fishes. They may be cultured in a similar manner as that of *Daphnia*.

4. Earth Worms: Small and tender chopped earthworms are used as good food for all aquarium fishes. Earthworms can be collected from your own backyard/garden where the soil is always moist.

5. Infusoria: The term Infusoria include minute microscopic organisms like Slipper Animalcule (*Paramecium*), Rotifers (*Brachionus*), (Fig. 21), etc., that breeds in water containing infusion of plant leaves. Infusoria have been used to feed very small fish larvae such as that of *Betta*, Dwarf Gourami and Glass Perch.

Fig. 21

Infusoria cultures can be raised very easily. As the first step, crushed and decaying vegetation, hay and yeast are added to a bowl or tank containing water. The decomposing vegetative matter will provide bacterial food for the developing infusoria. Water containing infusoria is now added to the culture tank. The entire tank will be filled with infusoria within 5 to 7 days, which can be fed directly to the young fishes.

6. Mosquito Larvae (Fig. 22): Mosquito larvae can be collected easily from stagnant water bodies containing decaying organic matter. Due to its smaller size (5 mm), fish can swallow them easily. Mosquito larvae collected from unhygienic places should be washed thoroughly before given as feed. An active aquarium fish can eat its own weight of mosquito larvae in the course of one day. Many aquarium fishes like Guppies, Paradise fish, etc are used for controlling mosquito larvae.

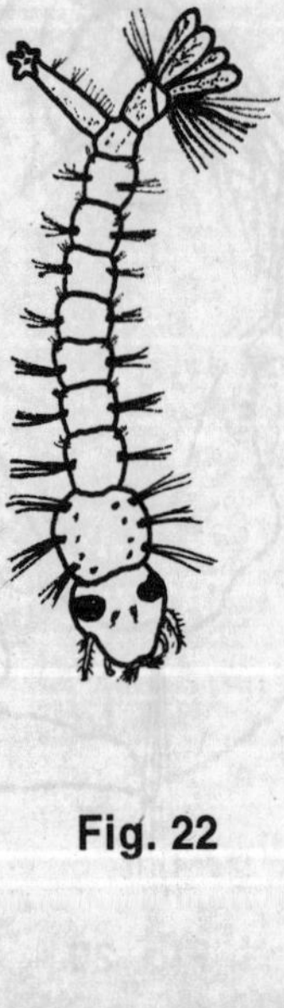

Fig. 22

7. Tubifex Worms: These are the most popular aquarium feed, commonly found in large numbers in sewage polluted waters. They must be thoroughly washed before use. Tubifex worms can be kept in live condition by placing it in a stream of water.

8. Other Natural Foods: Algae growing on rocks and stones in freshwater and aquarium plants like duckweed serve as food for fishes like Goldfish, Gouramies, Mollies, etc. Green water (*Chlorella*) and egg yolk infusions are better for newly hatched fishes. Direct addition of egg yolk may pollute aquarium water. To avoid this, take boiled egg yolk in a muslin cloth, immerse it in water and squeeze it gently till the required amount is dispersed in the water. Other commonly used live food material in aquaria are : *Cyclops*, Fairy shrimp (*Chirocephalus*), freshwater shrimp (*Gammarus*), glass worms (larvae of *Chaoborus* fly), Gridinal worms, micro worms and white worms (*Enchytrae*).

3.10.2. Artificial Food

In aquarium keeping one cannot depend wholly on natural food since their ready and steady supply cannot be ensured always. Today, high protein prepared food of varying forms (flakes, granular, pelleted, powdered and liquid) are available in the market to suit the varying needs of the aquarists. In addition, freeze-dried natural food materials like *Daphnia*, tubifex worms and brine shrimps are also available in the market. Alternating live food with artificial food was found to be better for the healthy growth of the fishes.

The artificial feed for aquarium fishes could be prepared in your own home. Based on the practical experience, the authors forward a recipe for preparing high protein feed for aquarium fishes.

	Ingredients	***Quantity***
1.	Dried fish (powdered)	250 gm
2.	Dried prawn (powdered)	200 gm
3.	Oil cake	200 gm
4.	Rice/Wheat bran	180 gm
5.	Soya bean/Wheat flour	150 gm
6.	Tapioca flour	20 gm
7.	Fish oil	20 ml
8.	Egg	4 nos

All the ingredients except fish oil are mixed well and the mixture is kneaded thoroughly adding minimum quantity of water to make a dough. The dough may be cooked for 30 minutes in steam, preferably in a pressure cooker. The dough is then allowed to cool. Add fish oil and powdered multivitamin multimineral tablets, if necessary. Mix thoroughly. Small pellets of required size could be prepared by passing it through a pelletizer with sieve of varying pore size. The pellets can be dried and stored in air tight containers for a long time. Aquarium fishes seem to respond well to this prepared food.

Feeding schedule for young fishes is given in the Table II.

Table II: Feeding Schedule for Baby Fishes (Fry)

	Food for the fry				
Size of fry	**First stage**	**Second stage**	**Third stage**	**Fourth stage**	**Fifth stage**
Small (eg : Bettas, Gouramies)	Green water.	Prepared dry food	Infusoria	Brine shrimps Large infusorians	Small dry food small Daphnia Large Daphnia
Medium (eg: Barbs, characins)	Egg yolk, Infusoria (small)	Small dry food, Rotifers	Brine shrimp, small clado cerans	Large dry food	Large Daphnia, chopped worms Large dry food
Large (eg: Live bearers, cichlids)	Brine shrimp nauplii, small dry food	Small Daphnia	Large cladocerans	Chopped worms Large dry food	Chopped worms Large dry food

3.11. Maintenance of Aquarium

Aquarium should be properly maintained in order to keep it balanced and healthy. The following tips should be kept in mind for maintaining a healthy aquarium.

1. Temperature of water should be checked and regulated daily in areas where there is drastic variation in daily temperature.
2. If you notice an oil film on the surface, remove it immediately since this prevents atmospheric oxygen from dissolving into the water. The oil can be removed by spreading a sheet of news paper on the surface and towing it gently.
3. Diseased fishes, fishes showing disease symptoms and dead fishes, if any, should be removed from the aquarium tank. It is advisable to use hand nets, preferably rectangular ones, to catch/remove fishes from the tank.
4. Remove the uneaten food and waste products periodically. It can be done either by using a small hose or by using a vacuum cleaner. The suction head of the hose should be atleast 1 cm above the bottom in order to avoid the removal of gravel or sand.
5. In order to maintain stable water conditions, partial water change (10 - 25 % of the total water content) in every two to three weeks is recommended.

6. Growth of algae on aquarium glass can be prevented by periodically cleaning the glass panes using a razor blade scraper or magnetic algae cleaners. If these equipments are not available, soaked clean cotton cloth tied at one end of a rod may be used for removing the algae. Rusty brown algae are often difficult to eliminate. Application of common salt is supposed to be efficient in controlling the growth of this algae. If there is heavy blooming of algae of any kind, it is better to remove fishes and clean the water completely followed by disinfecting the tank with dilute Copper sulphate solution. Light blooms may be controlled either by introducing *Daphnia* (after removing fishes) or by diluting the water.

7. The working conditions of aerator, filter and heater should be checked periodically. The cleaning medium contained in filters (charcoal and cotton) should be replaced if needed. If there is some kind of interruption in the flow of water in biological filters, it can be corrected by rearranging the gravel. Blocked air stones in aerators may be rectified by placing them in boiled water.

8. Avoid sudden switching off and on of aquarium light since this may directly interfere with the normal behaviour of fishes. Switch off and switch on the aquarium light when room light is present.

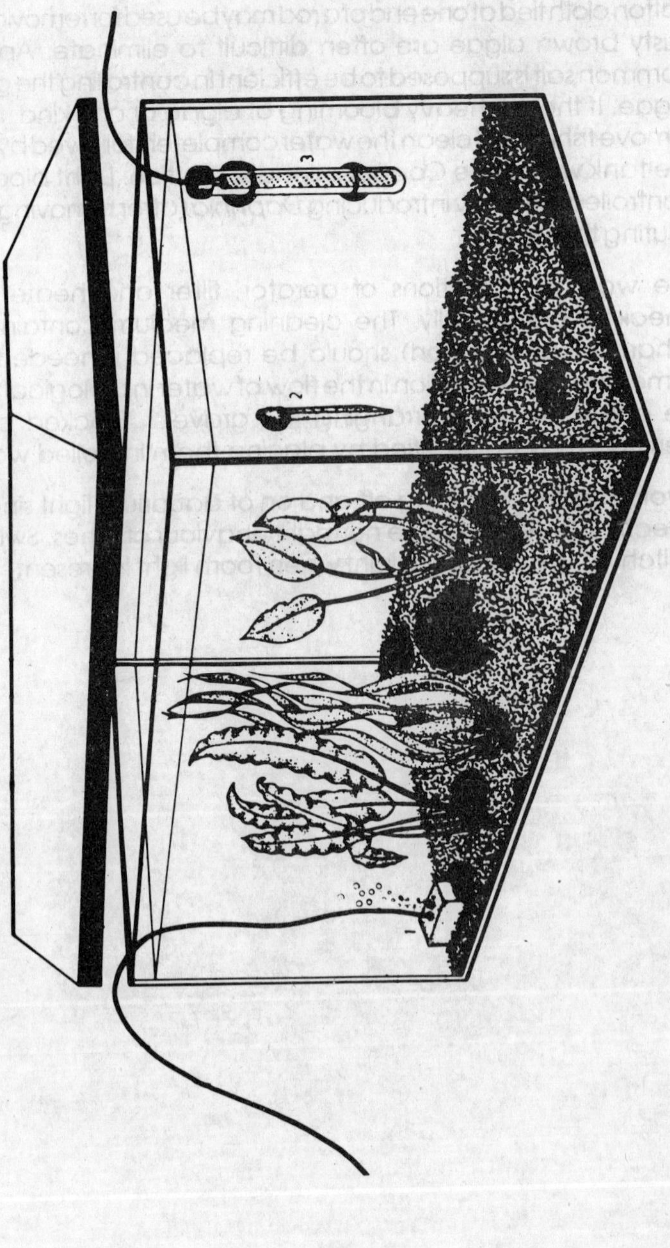

Fig. 22a Set-up of the Home Aquarium.
1. Filter 2. Thermometer 3. Heater

COMMON AQUARIUM FISHES

Aquarium fishes can be generally classified into egg layers and live bearers.

4.1. Egg Layers

Egg laying fishes hatch their young ones from eggs. Important egg laying fishes are the following:

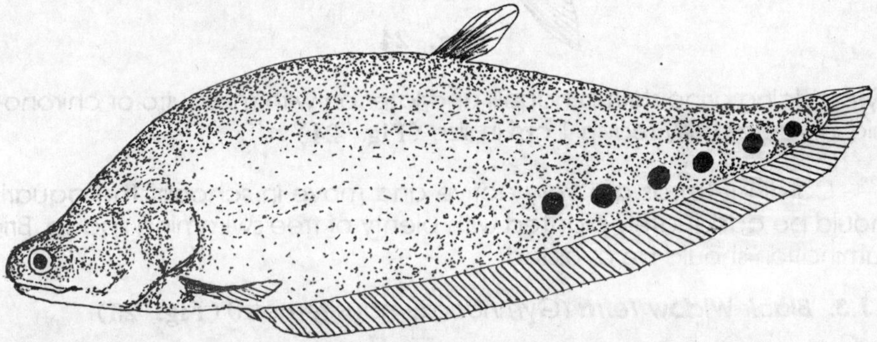

Fig. 23

4.1.1. Knife Fish (Notopterus chitala)

The knife fish commonly inhabit the rivers of India. The body is compressed and elongated like a knife. The fish grows to 80 cm in size. Often other fishes form its main food item. Hence it is better not to keep the knife fishes with fishes smaller than them. Aquarium breeding is rather difficult. The adult fishes are often solitary. Bright illumination should be avoided in the aquarium (Fig. 23).

4.1.2. Cardinal Tetra (Cheirodon axelrodi)

It is the most beautiful of aquarium fishes. Cardinal tetra is native to South America. They have uninterrupted horizontal streaks of electric blue and red on its sides. It grows to 4 cm in size. This fish feed on small insect larvae and fishes in the wild, but responds well to prepared feed. Aquarium breeding is by providing adequate environmental conditions for the fish to spawn. Female fishes can be identified by the presence of a fuller belly. Spawning is induced by a rise in atmospheric pressure. They spawn only when kept together for 2 to 3 weeks. The eggs hatch in a day's time and the newly hatched fry remain behind plant thickets. The fry can be nourished

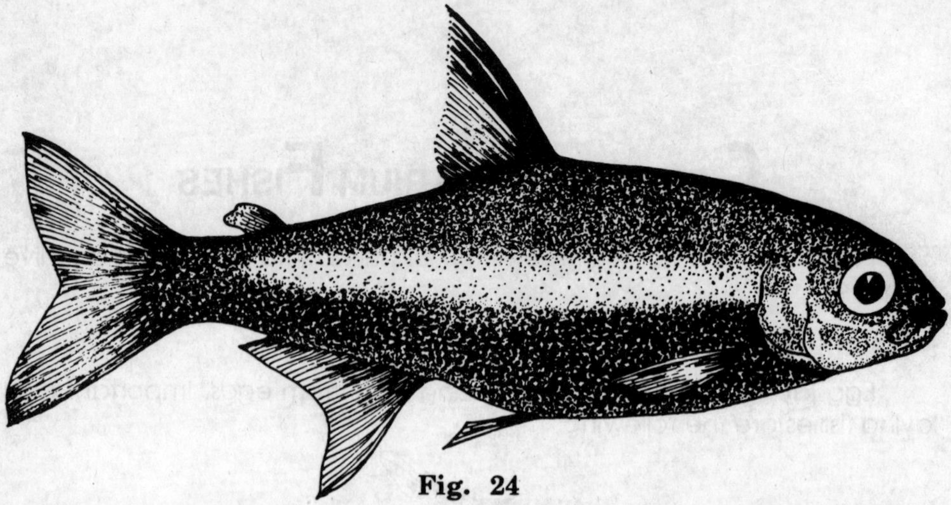

Fig. 24

by providing brine shrimp nauplii and later on with mosquito or chironomid larvae as they reach 1 cm in size (Fig. 24).

Cardinal Tetras are very active and move in schools. The aquarium should be adequately planted with plenty of free swimming space. Bright illumination should be avoided.

4.1.3. Black Widow Tetra *(Gymnocoxymbus ternetzi)* (Fig. 25)

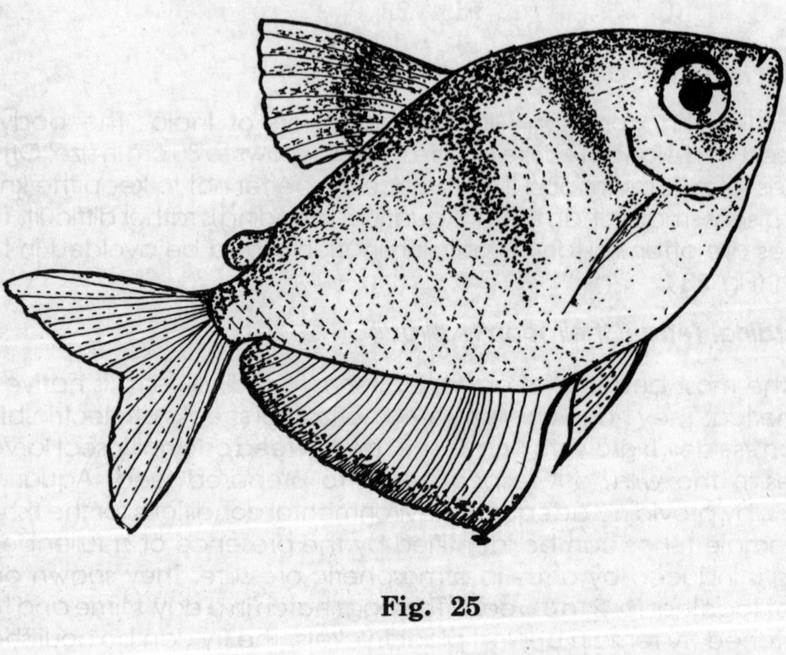

Fig. 25

Black Widow Tetras inhabit freshwater bodies of South America. When young, the fish is very attractive, with the posterior half of the body and the large anal and caudal fins black in colour. The body also possess two distinct vertical incomplete black bars across the abdomen. But as the fish grows, the body colour fades to a dull grey. This fish grows to 5 cm in size. Their main food comprises of algae and other live organisms, but they readily adapt themselves to prepared food.

This fish can easily be bred in the aquarium. Males are darker, with elongated dorsal fins. It is advisable to use spawning grids, but in its absence a well planted tank should be provided with the bottom covered with pebbles or marble. The spawners should be removed as soon as spawning is over. The eggs hatch in 24 hours and the fry are fed with infusoria and *Artemia* nauplii.

Black Widow Tetras prefer diffused light. They are peaceable and could be kept in a community tank.

4.1.4. Buenos Aires Tetra*(Hemigrammus caudovittatus)*

Buenos Aires Tetra has its origin in the La Plata region of Argentina. The laterally compressed body is silvery in appearance with fins red in colour. The posterior tip of the body has a large black diamond-shaped marking which extends upto the tip of the caudal fin. The fish grows to a size of 10 cm (Fig. 26).

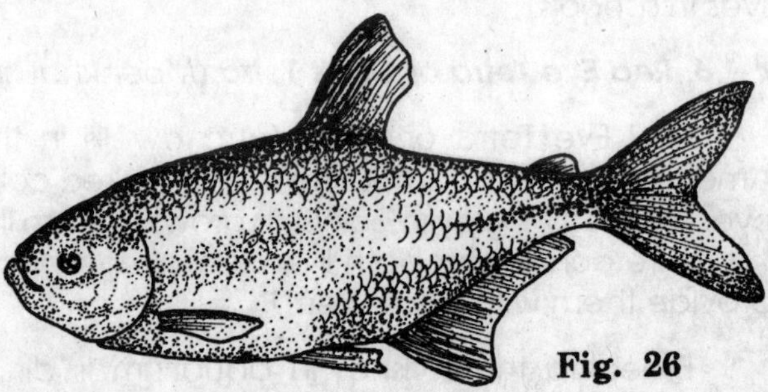

Fig. 26

The fins of males are deeper orange red than the female and the abdomen is fuller and more curved in the female. It is a prolific breeder and the female lays 80 to 150 eggs in one spawning. The eggs are scattered among the plants. The adults should be removed as soon as spawning is over and water level reduced to 10 cm. Spawning grids may be used to protect the eggs from being eaten by the parents themselves. The eggs hatch in 2 to 3 days time and the fry cling on the plants. The fry has to be fed with infusoria as soon as they become free swimming.

A red eyed albinotic (white) form has also been available.

4.1.5. Serpae Tetra *(Hyphessobrycon serpae)* (Fig. 27)

Serpae Tetra originate from the Amazon basin of South America. It has a glowing red body with yellowish abdomen. An elongated black blotch is present above the belly. The fish grows to 4.5 cm in size. Serpae Tetra is an omnivorous feeder and can easily adjust to the artificial feed. Males are bright red in colour with belly less curved than in female. They are egg scatterers. The minute grey coloured eggs hatch in 24 hours. The fry can be fed with brine shrimp larvae. Serpae Tetra is a very peaceable fish which lives in schools.

Fig. 27

4.1.6. Red Eye Tetra or Glass Tetra *(Moenkhausia sanctaefilomenae)*

Red Eye Tetra or Glass Tetra dwells in the water bodies of South America. The fish is famous for the flashy red colour in the upper half of the eye. The body is grey in colour. It grows to 7 cm in size. The fish is omnivorous in nature consuming both live animal and plant matter. Once in a while provide them with Duck Weed.

Breeding these fishes in aquarium is difficult. Females have more rounded and curved belly. The breeding pair has to be conditioned two weeks prior to spawning. Eggs hatch in 24 hours. The fry feed on infusoria in early stages, followed by brine shrimp larvae and water flea.

The young ones grow very slowly. The aquarium should be dimly lit with one-third vegetation and the rest free swimming space. It can be kept with other schooling fishes due to its peaceful nature.

4.1.7. Neon Tetra *(Paracheirodon innesi)* (Fig. 28)

Neon Tetra widely occurs in the slow moving rivers of South America. The body is coloured in shades of electric blue and red. The streak of electric red is incomplete at the abdominal region which is almost white in colour. They grow to 4 cm in size. The fish thrives well in soft acidic waters of pH 6 - 6.5 and temperature around 21°C.

Aquarium breeding is possible, but not easy. Females are more plump and a bend is visible in the electric blue line along the flanks. Prior to spawning, males and females have to be kept in separate tanks for two weeks in cooler waters of temperature around 19°C. Sterilized peat extract should be added to the breeding water. Parents are to be removed as soon as spawning is over. Since the developing embryos prefer dim light, the breeding tank should be properly covered.

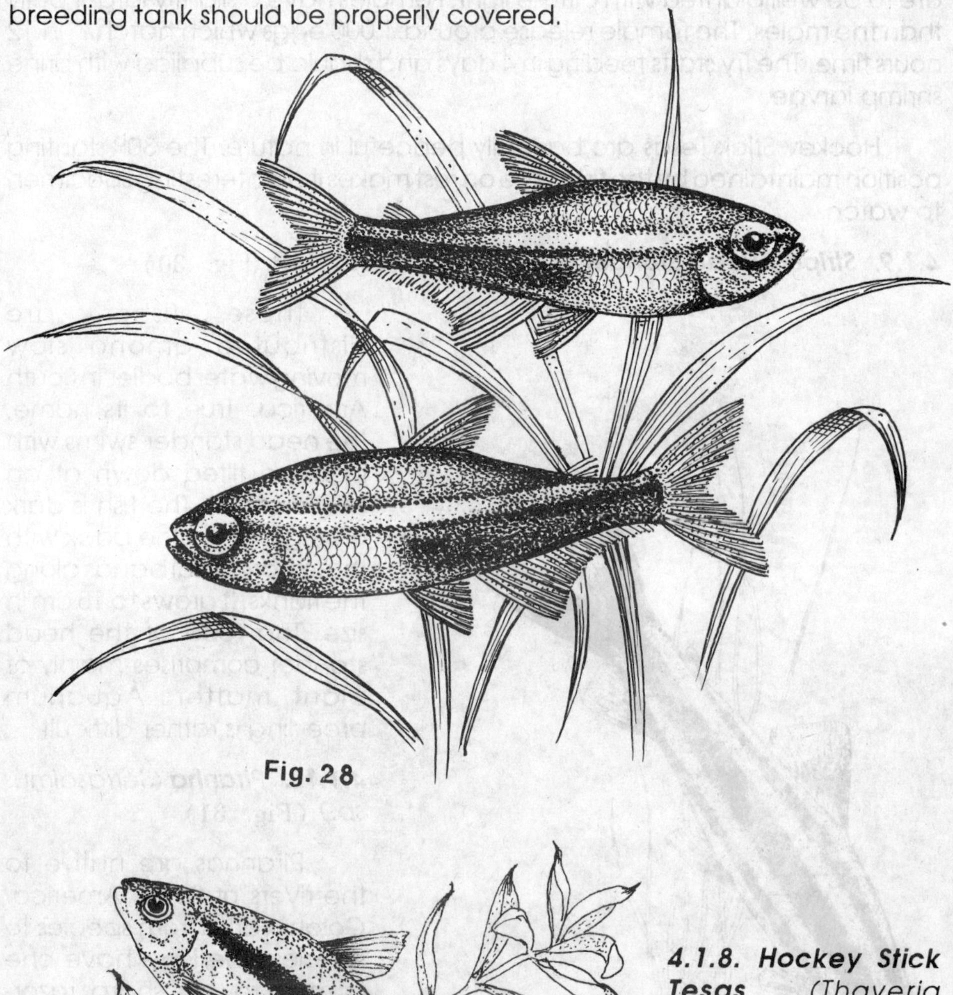

Fig. 28

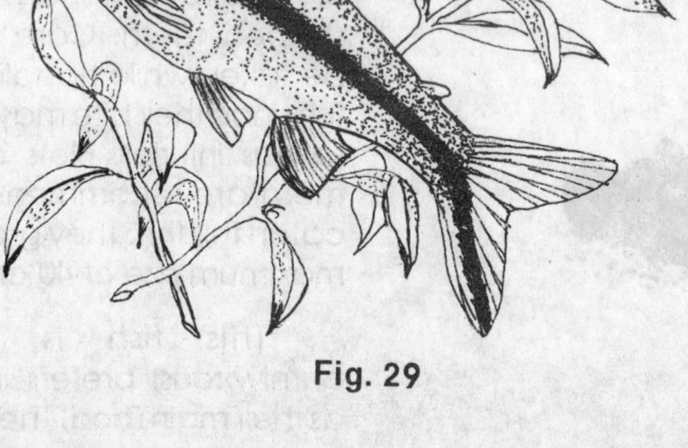

Fig. 29

4.1.8. Hockey Stick Tesas *(Thayeria boehlkei)* (Fig. 29)

The Hockey-stick Tesas,an inhabitant of Brazil and Peru, owes its name to a black line which runs through the entire body and continues down the lower lobe of the caudal fin. It grows to 6 cm in size. It is omnivorous and responds well to artificial feed.

Breeding these fishes in aquarium is possible, but the breeding tanks are to be well planted with diffuse light. Females have a slightly larger belly than the males. The female release around 1,000 eggs which hatch in 12 hours time. The fry starts feeding in 4 days and should be supplied with brine shrimp larvae.

Hockey Stick Tesas are basically peaceful in nature. The 30° slanting position maintained by the fish while on rest makes it an interesting specimen to watch.

4.1.9. Striped Head Stander *(Anostomus anostomus)* (Fig. 30)

These fishes are distributed among slow moving water bodies in South America. True to its name, the head stander swims with its head tilted down at an angle of 45°. The fish is dark olive green on the back with three horizontal bands along the flanks. It grows to 15 cm in size. The food of the head stander comprises mainly of plant matter. Aquarium breeding is rather difficult.

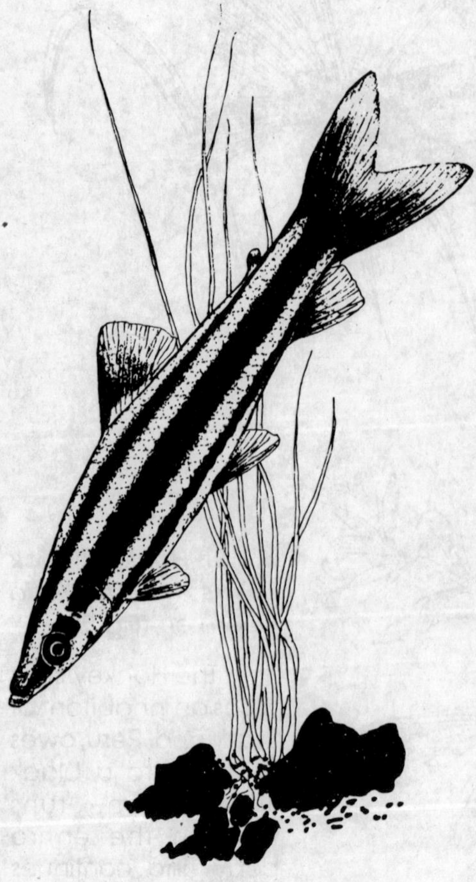

Fig. 30

4.1.10. Piranha *(Serrasalmus sp.)* (Fig. 31)

Piranhas are native to the rivers of South America. Colour varies from species to species. The jaws have one or more rows of sharp, razor-shaped teeth. Care should be taken while handling the fish since their bite may cause serious injuries. Nets of wire mesh are recommended to catch this fish. They grow to a maximum size of 40 cm.

This fish is highly carnivorous; prefers live fish as their main food. They are

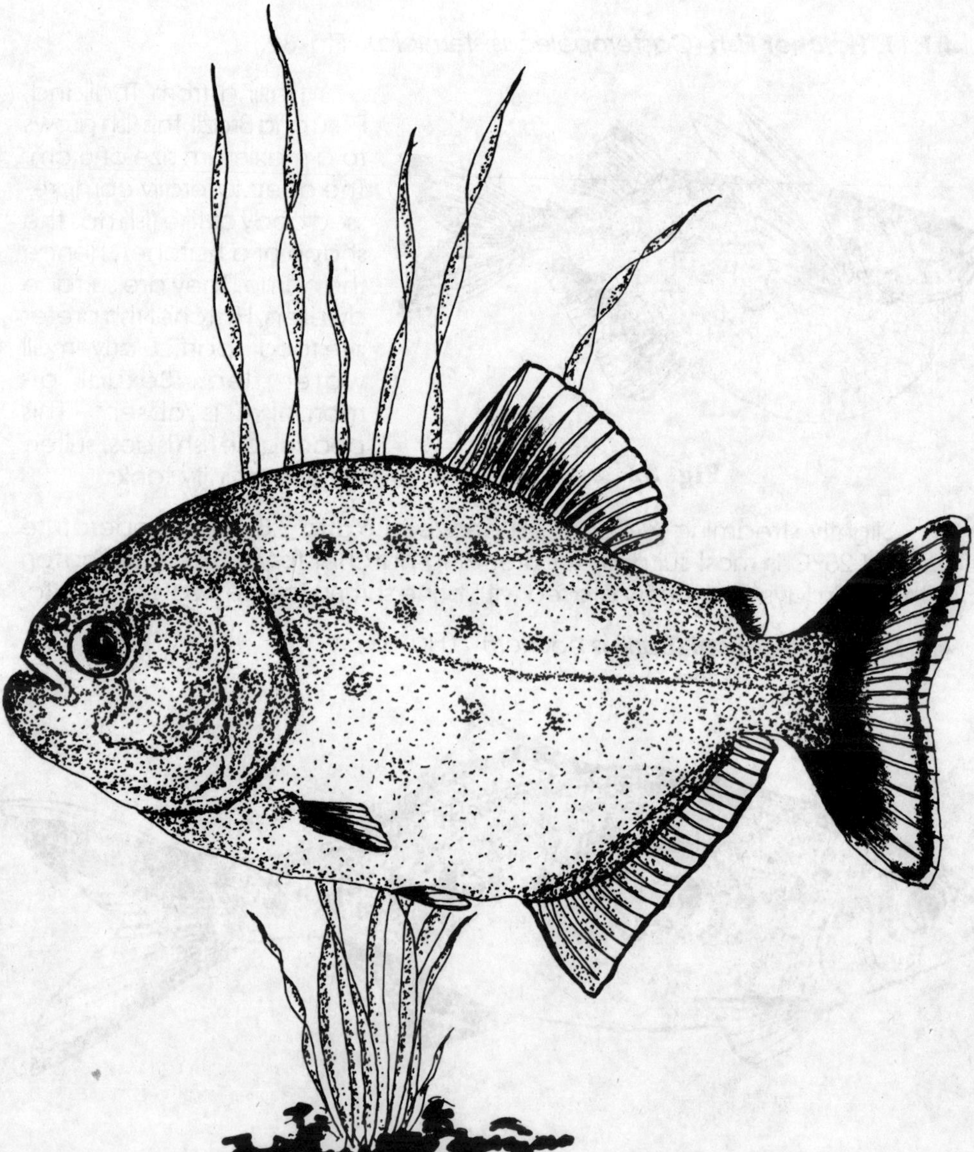

Fig. 31

always kept in monospecies tank. Piranhas are voracious feeders. It is always better to feed them continuously, lest they attack each other. Sexual differentiation is rather difficult.

Large tanks are necessary for breeding purpose. Male fish makes small pits in the bottom and guard the egg till hatching. 300-400 eggs are laid at a particular time. The developed embryos should be removed to another tank. During growth it is advisable to separate them according to their size in order to prevent them from attacking each other.

4.1.11. Hatchet Fish *(Gasteropelecus sternicla)* (Fig. 32)

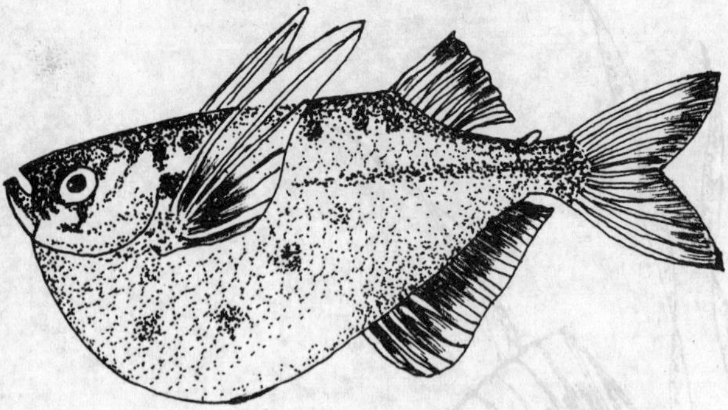

Fig. 32

Hailing from Thailand, Peru and Brazil, this fish grows to a maximum size of 6 cm. The deep, laterally compressed body of the fish has the shape of a hatchet, hence the name. They are surface dwellers. Hatchet fish prefer live food , particularly small water flea. Sexual dimorphism is absent. This peaceable fish is best suited for community tanks.

Slightly streaming water of pH between 6.5 to 7.0 and temperature around 25°C is most suitable for breeding hatchet fishes. The eggs hatch within two days and the fry are fed with brine shrimp larvae, water flea, etc.

4.1.12. Malabar Baril *(Barilius backeri)* (Fig. 33)

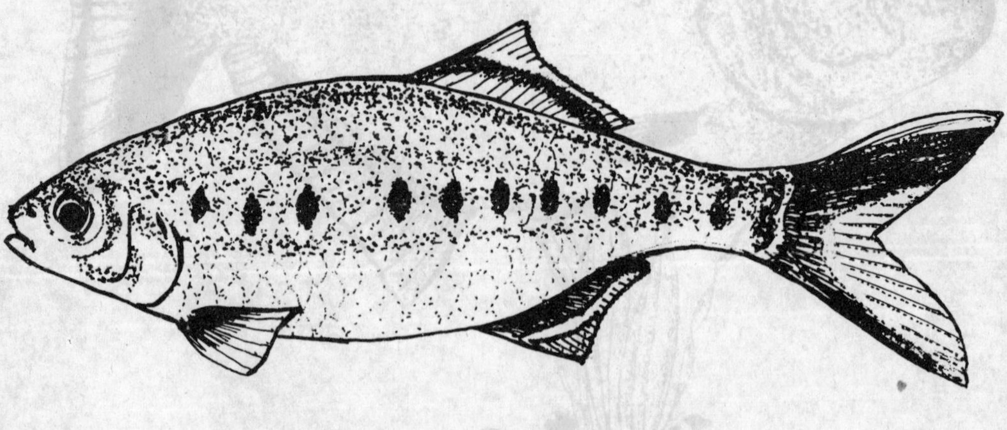

Fig. 33

This fast swimming fish comes from the hill streams of south India. The olive green body bears a horizontal row of bluish spots across the flanks. It grows to a size of 15 cm. They require water of pH around 7.0 and temperature between 22 and 25°c. They readily accept artificial feed but food must be scattered on the water surface since they are surface feeders.

There is lack of the information regarding their breeding habits and sex determination.

4.1.13. Zebra Danio
(Brachydanio rerio)

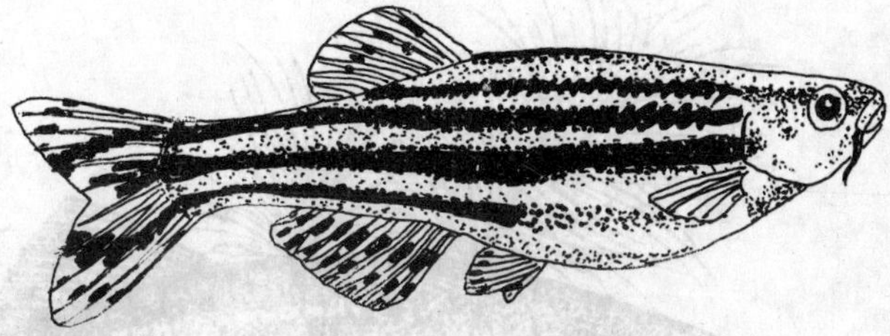

Fig. 34

This active little beauty hails from fast flowing and shallow streams of North Eastern India. It is highly valued for its metallic blue and silvery gold horizontal stripes across its flanks. It grows to 5 cm in size. They are surface feeders preying mainly on insects, but readily accept artificial feed. In a community tank care must be taken to scatter some food on the surface for the Danios, since they are surface feeders (Fig. 34).

Aquarium breeding is easy. The fishes should be separated and conditioned for a week on mosquito larvae or tubifex worms. It is very easy to distinguish the sex. Males are smaller and slimmer. For breeding purpose, the fishes are introduced into the breeding tank in the ratio 2/3 :1 (two to three males for a female), in order to achieve better results. The female lays almost 1,000 eggs at a time. The water level should be very low and the bottom completely covered with pebbles, in case spawning grids are not available. As soon as the spawning is over, remove the parents. A good supply of clean water is necessary for successful hatching. The incubation period of eggs is 60 hours. Hatching is always hastened by a rise in temperature. The fry can be reared on green water (*Chlorella*) and boiled egg yolk.

4.1.14. Leopard Danio *(Brachydanio frankei)*

Leopard Danio is very much similar to Zebra Danio in appearance, except for the fact that the former has got blue spots on the flanks. *B. frankei* is a mutant form of *B. rerio* and frequently interbreeds with the latter. Water quality requirements, food and spawning procedures are same as that of Zebra Danio. But, spawning this species is not an easy affair as that of Zebra Danios due to the presence of large number of unfertilized eggs.

4.1.15. Giant Danio *(Danio malabaricus)*

Giant Danio is the native of southern India and Sri Lanka. The body is metallic turquoise blue with a pinkish belly. It grows to a maximum length of 12 cm. In aquarium they respond well to prepared food. Breeding is generally similar to Zebra Danio.

They are peaceable schooling fishes, always on the move. They are very good community tank fishes (Fig. 35).

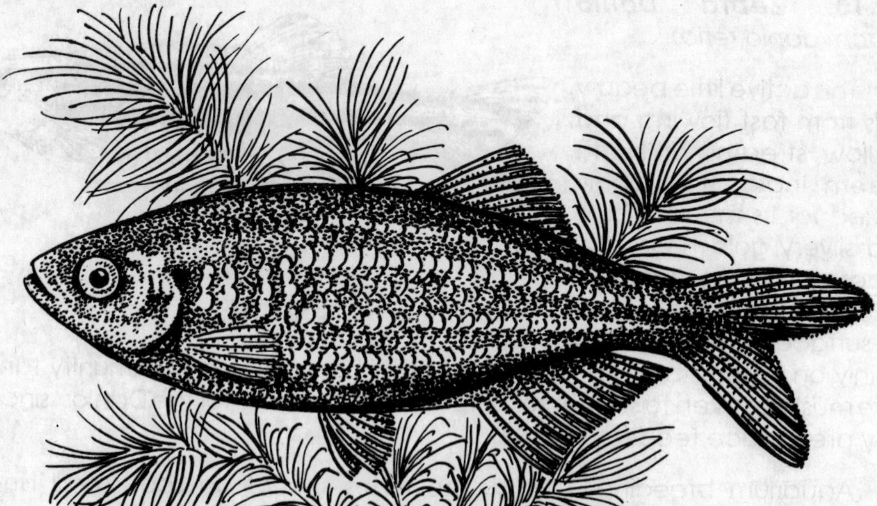

Fig. 35

4.1.16. Flying Barb (*Esomus danrica*)

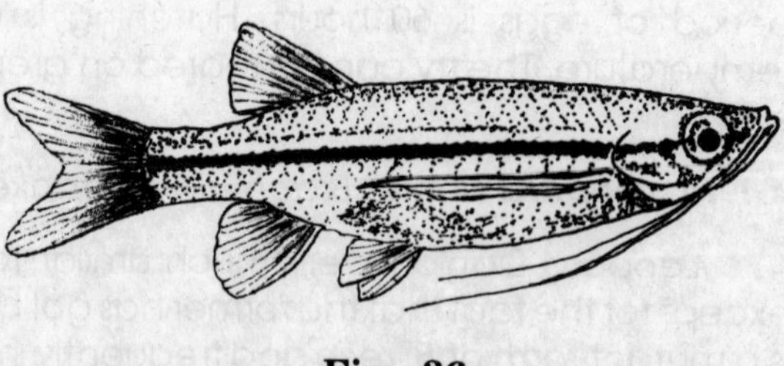

Fig. 36

The flying barb has its origin in India and Sri Lanka. The silvery body of this fish is divided from the olive green back by a dark horizontal line extending from the mouth to caudal peduncle. They have two pairs of barbels; the lower pair being long reaching the middle of the body. The pectoral fins are much elongated, enabling the fish to leap out of water and glide short distances. They attain a body length of 10 cm. In the aquarium they can be reared on a diet of chopped earth worms or artificial food (Fig. 36).

A large thickly planted aquarium with water column around 15 cm should be provided for breeding. A layer of pebbles should be kept at the bottom. The males are smaller and slender than the females. Before spawning, the pair should be separated for two weeks and conditioned on a diet of live feed. Spawning takes place at dawn. The fertilized eggs are partially sticky and may fall to the bottom of the tank among the pebbles. The parents are to be removed immediately after spawning. The water level has to be lowered to 5 cm. The eggs hatch within a day and infusoria should be provided as food for the free swimming larvae. This can be later replaced by brine shrimp nauplii. Keep the aquarium covered as these fishes are expert jumpers. It is a good community fish.

4.1.17. Long Fin Barb *(Puntius arulius)*

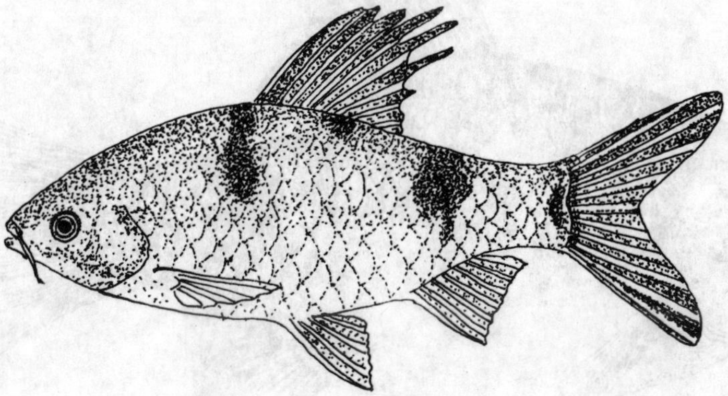

Fig. 37

The long fin barb is one of the largest barbs inhabiting the freshwater bodies of India. It has a silvery body with olive green colour on the back. The dorsal, anal and caudal fins are pinkish red in colour. The size of a fully grown specimen may reach upto 14 cm in length. Food comprises mainly of vegetable materials but they easily adapt to prepared food **(Fig. 37).**

In the mature males the dorsal fin rays are elongated and the body colour become more intense. Spawning takes place during dusk among plant thickets. The brown coloured eggs stick to the plants. The spawners have to be removed as soon as spawning is over. The eggs hatch in 40 hours and the fry attach themselves to glass panes and leaves of aquatic plants. As soon as they start to swim freely, they can be fed with brine shrimp larvae and later on with water flea.

Long finn barb is very active and needs a large aquarium. Care must be taken to provide them with a regular supply of cooked cabbage or spinach to stop them from feeding on soft aquarium plants.

4.1.18. Rosy Barb *(Puntius conchonius)* (Fig. 38)

This little beauty from the northern India is perfect for the home aquarium. The body of the wild Rosy Barb is green with rose belly. The fins are yellowish and both sexes have a black spot above the anal fin. It grows to 12 cm in size. Breeding is similar to that of long fin barb.

Rosy barb is a very active and hardy community fish. They are available in three other forms also. These include the smaller golden coloured variety of the Rosy barb and the veil finned varieties of both Rosy barb and the golden variety of the same.

Fig. 38

4.1.19. Black Spot Barb *(Puntius filamentosus)*

This species inhabits the fast flowing turbid streams of south India and Sri Lanka. The body has got a metallic shade of golden silver with a tear-shaped black spot above the anal fin. Adult fishes grow to about 15 cm in length. The food of this fish mainly include insect larva (Fig. 39).

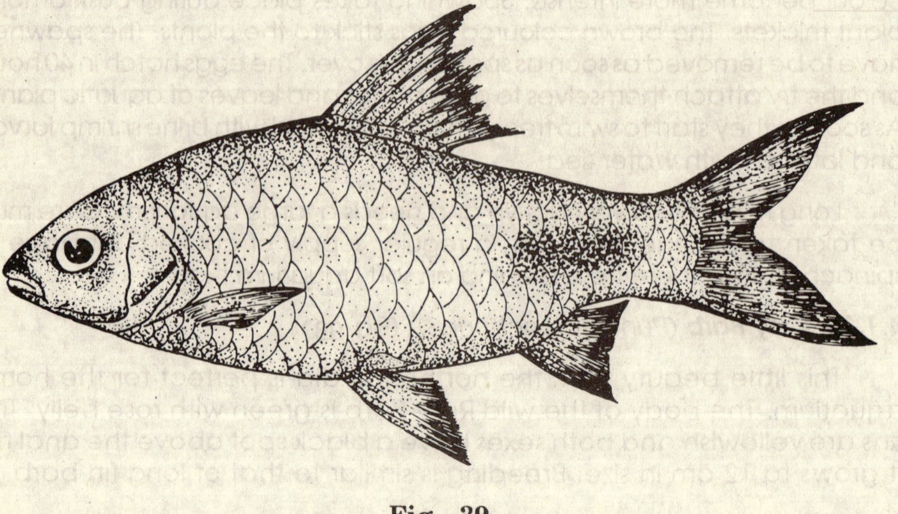

Fig. 39

Mature males develop small spawning tubercles on the snout. Males can also be distinguished by the extended dorsal fin rays and deeper colouration on the fins. Aquarium breeding is difficult. Spawning takes place among aquatic plants in the surface. The yellowish brown eggs stick on to the leaves and roots of plants. The eggs hatch in 48 hours. The fry should be fed with brine shrimp larvae and later on with water flea.

The Black Spot Barb is a very hardy fish, suited very much for a community aquarium. Try to provide as large an aquarium as possible, since the fish needs plenty of swimming space.

4.1.20. Melon Barb *(Puntius melanampyx)*

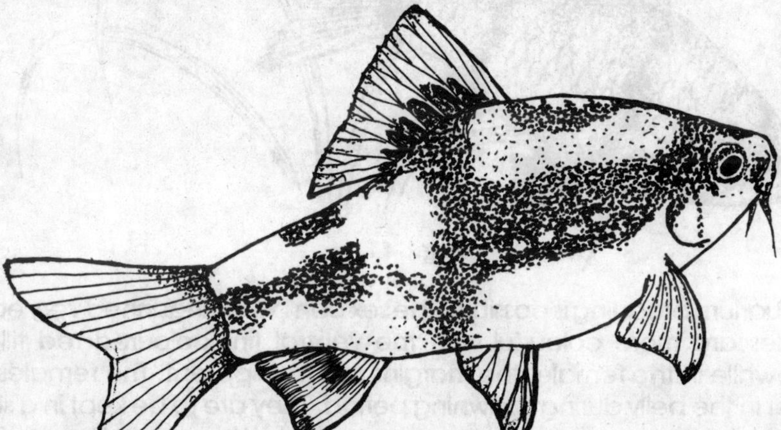

Fig. 40

Melon Barb is the inhabitant of the hill streams of southern India. It has a pinkish brown body with vertical black bands across its body. Melon barbs are much smaller than the Black Spot Barbs and grow to 5 cm in size.

They are bottom feeders and their main food include chironomid larvae, tubifex worms etc. In the aquarium they readily accept any artificial feed (Fig. 40).

Aquarium breeding has not been tried yet. Melon barbs are hardy and peaceful. The aquarium should be moderately planted with sufficient light.

4.1.21. Tiger Barb *(Puntius tetrazona)*

This fish, native of Indonesia, has a pinkish yellow body with four definite vertical black bands, one of which passes through the eye. Tiger barb grows to 7.5 cm in size. They thrive well on a diet of tubifex worms as well as artificial food (Fig. 41).

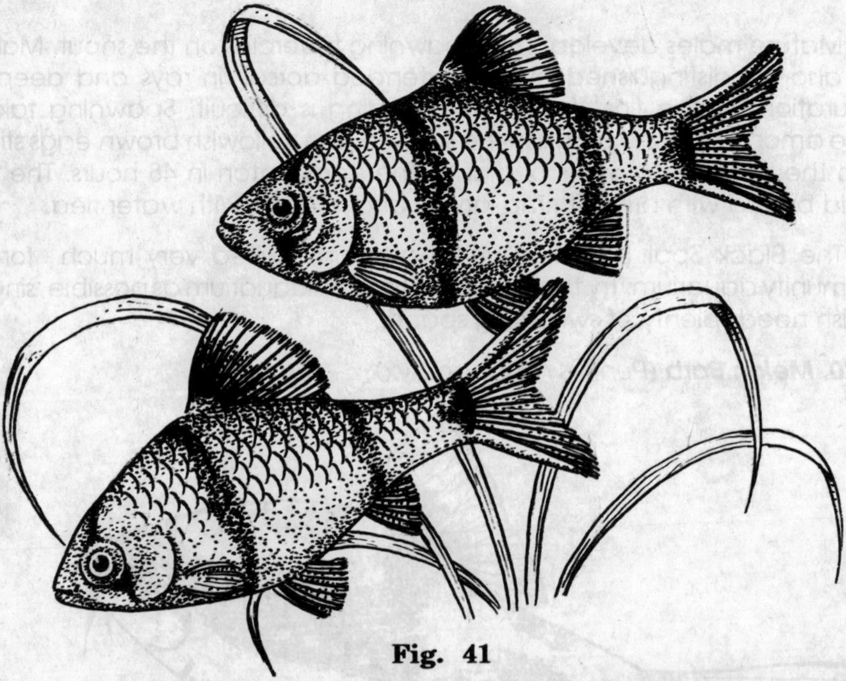

Fig. 41

Aquarium breeding is possible. The sex can be distinguished very easily. The males are more colourful with the ventral fins coloured red till the margin, while in the female, the margins are transparent. The females are also fuller in the belly during spawning period. They are to be kept in a shoal in a relatively large aquarium for spawning. The bottom should be covered with marble and adequately planted. Addition of peat extract is advisable. The adults have to be removed as soon as spawning is over and water level reduced to 10 cm. The eggs have to be treated with a weak solution of Methylene blue to prevent fungal attack. The incubation period is 36 hours and the fry can be nourished by providing them with a culture of brine shrimp larvae. The young fishes grow very fast till they reach 1 cm in size. At this stage, they are prone to infections. After this critical phase is over they are quite hardy.

Always keep them in large groups because fishes kept in small numbers tend to fight among themselves. Care must be taken not to include small fishes and those with long delicate fins like gold fish, as Tiger barbs have the habit of nipping their fins.

4.1.22. Slender Rasbora *(Rasbora daniconius)*

The Slender Rasbora dwells in almost all types of freshwater bodies in India and Sri Lanka. The fish has a slender and elongated body with a round abdomen. The body is medium olive colour with a greenish sheen in the silvery belly. A distinct horizontal blue-black band bordered with gold patches from the head to the base of the caudal fin. Slender Rasbora is a large fish often reaching 15 cm in length. It is a hardy fish and can tolerate wide fluctuations in pH and temperature. They can easily be reared on artificial feed (Fig. 42).

Fig. 42

The breeding tank should be moderately planted with sufficient swimming space. The bottom should have a layer of marble or pebbles as a precaution to save the eggs from being eaten. The sex can be distinguished during the spawning season by the presence of a fuller belly in the female. They scatter the eggs which are collected between the pebbles. The parents are to be removed immediately after the spawning is over. The eggs hatch in 36 to 40 hours. Rearing of the fry is the same as with Danios.

The aquarium should be well covered to protect these expert jumpers from leaping out.

4.1.23. Gold Fish *(Carassius auratus)* (Fig. 43)

The Gold Fish originated from East Asia, Siberia and China. Gold fish grows to 45 cm in the wild. The fish can tolerate wide fluctuations in pH and hardness. It is omnivorous in feeding habits and can survive on both live as well as dried animal and vegetable matter. Gold fish is very peaceful and is best suited for the community tank.

The males are generally slender than the females. But rounder males are also not uncommon. Hence, the only reliable method of distinguishing the sex is by the presence of small sand like projections (tubercles) on the operculum of males after maturation.

Before breeding, the male and female should be kept in the same tank with a glass partition in between and conditioned for a week. During this period, the fish should be fed on live chopped earth worms, tubifex worms or minced meat and liver. The temperature in conditioning tank should be raised gradually to 4 degrees above the breeding tank. The spawners after conditioning are to be released to the breeding tank by dusk. It is advisable to use two or three males for a single female to ensure higher fertilisation rate of eggs. The breeding tank should be densely

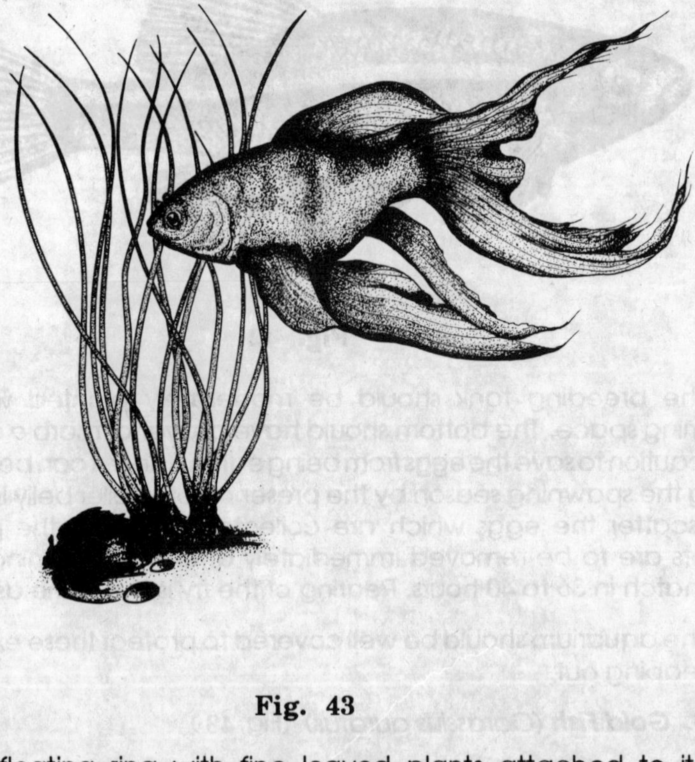

Fig. 43

planted. A floating ring with fine leaved plants attached to it, may also be provided. The spawning process usually takes place by dawn. The eggs released by the female are fertilised by the male. The adhesive, gelatinous eggs stick on to the plants. The plants with eggs can be transferred to a nursery tank with water level around 20 cm. The eggs hatch in 3 to 5 days. The fry cling on to plants by sucking action. The fish may be fed on fine infusoria as they reach the free swimming stage. Later it can be supplemented with fine egg yolk. Four week old fishes should be fed with water flea.

4.1.24. Koi Carp (Cyprinus carpio)

Koi (the Japanese word for carp) is the native of Japan. The aquarium reared Koi is a colour variant of the common carp. Koi differs from goldfish in having two prominent barbels at the corner of its mouth. Koi is available in a whole range of colours and shades. The food of Koi include submerged plants and other benthic organisms. They readily accept artificial feed.

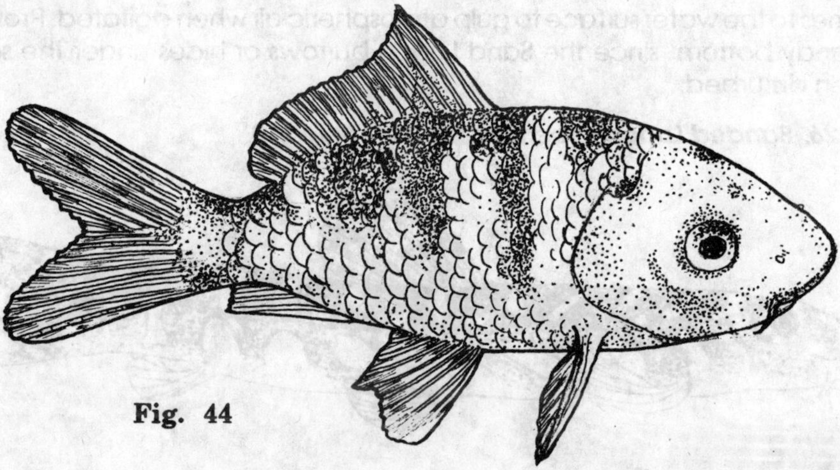

Fig. 44

Males have spawning tubercles while the females are more rounder when viewed from above. Koi become sexually mature by 2 to 4 years. Breeding technique is similar to that of gold fish. The incubation period of eggs is 3 to 5 days and the fry starts feeding by the 10th day (Fig. 44).

The fish needs a large aquarium with water colum above 150 cm. They constantly uproot the plants and muddy the water by digging the pond bottom. They are very peaceful and hardy.

4.1.25 Sand Loach *(Lepidocephalus thermalis)* (Fig. 45)

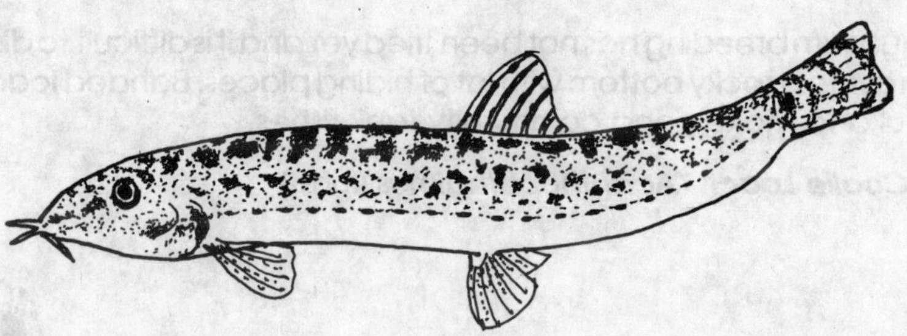

Fig. 45

The Sand loach inhabit streams, lakes and swamps of southern and central India. The elongated body of this fish is grey green in colour with 8 to 10 dark irregular blotches along the sides. Inferior mouth is surrounded by three pairs of barbel. Sand loach attains a length of 9 cm. They mainly feed on detritus and can be reared on a whole range of artificial feed.

They are monomorphic and details regarding their breeding habits are scarce. A peculiar behaviour exhibited by this fish is that it frequently comes to the water surface to gulp atmospheric air when agitated. Provide a sandy bottom since the Sand Loach burrows or hides under the sand when disturbed.

4.1.26. Banded Loach (*Noemacheilus triangularis*)

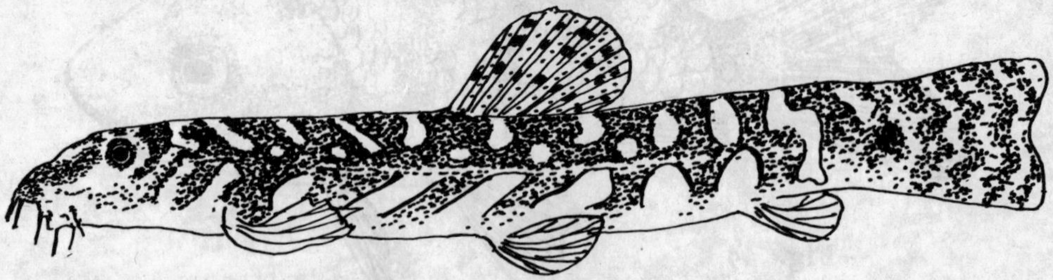

Fig. 46

The banded loach thrives in fast moving streams of southern India. Nearly 70 species of more or less similar looking *Noemacheilus* were recorded from India and hence it is very difficult to differentiate the species. Seven yellow bands margined with black are present on the body, as shown in the figure. A dark black blotch is present at the base of the caudal fin. Small inferior mouth is surrounded by four pairs of barbels. This fish attains a length of 6 cm. However, in the aquarium they can thrive well on artificial food (Fig. 46).

Aquarium breeding has not been tried yet and it is difficult to distinguish sexes. Provide a rocky bottom with lot of hiding places. Banded loaches are peaceful and make good community tank fishes.

4.1.27. Coolie Loach (*Acanthophthalmus kuhlii*)

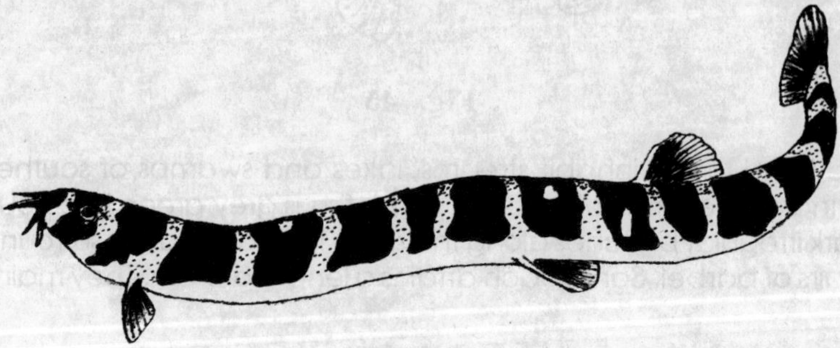

Fig. 47

Coolie loach thrives in the freshwater bodies of the southern part of the Malayan peninsula, Sumatra, Jawa and Borneo. It has an elongated slightly compressed body with small fins. The body has 15 to 20 black vertical bands on a pinkish yellow body. They possess 4 pairs of barbels. They attain a length of 8 cm (Fig. 47).

Sex can be determined during the breeding season, since the females become bulky before spawning. In the wild the fish spawn in shallow waters. Coolie loach can be kept in a community tank with non aggressive fishes. It is better to provide a thick layer of sand on the bottom since the fish burrows into the soft sand. Also try to provide enough hiding places.

4.1.28. Reticulated or 'Y' Loach *(Botia lohachata)* (Fig. 48)

Fig. 48

They inhabit the rivers of northern India. This fish possess a series of 'Y' shaped markings on both sides of the earthy brown body. It grows to a maximum of 10 cm. They feed on worms and other living organisms.

It is difficult to distinguish the sex, and information regarding aquarium breeding is scarce. Unlike other loaches, the 'Y' loach does not hide during day time. They can be kept in a community tank.

4.1.29. Indian Glass Catfish *(Kryptopterus bicirrhus)*

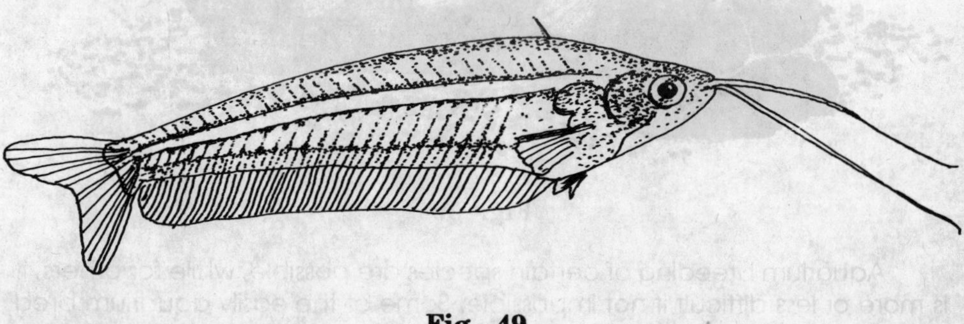

Fig. 49

This catfish inhabits the rivers of India and China. The body is transparent and hence the name. Unlike other catfishes, the Indian Glass Catfish frequents the upper layers of water. They prefer live food but can also thrive well on artificial feed (Fig. 49).

Males grow to a size of 10 cm and are smaller than the females. There is no information regarding aquarium rearing of this fish. The young ones and adults move in shoals and it is advisable not to keep the Glass Catfish alone, for it would soon pine away and die. The aquarium should be shallow and well planted since the fish has the habit of resting on plants at times.

4.1.30. Dwarf Catfishes

Dwarf catfishes include armoured catfishes inhabiting South America. The body is flattened on sides with an arched dorsal outline (see figure). The genus *Corydoras* (Fig. 50) form the major representative of this group. These fishes can survive in poorly oxygenated waters since they can utilise atmospheric air for respiration. They are peaceful schooling fishes.

Fig. 50

Aquarium breeding of certain species are possible, while for others, it is more or less difficult if not impossible. Some of the easily aquarium bred

Corydoras include the Network Catfish (*Corydoras reticulatus*), Schwartz Corydoras (*C. schwartzi*), Bronze Catfish (*C. aeneus*), Dwarf Corydoras (*C. rabauti*) and Pygmy Catfish (*C. hastatus*). The general spawning procedure of Corydoras is described here. However, there are slight variations among different species. Before spawning, these fishes swim in a shoal comprising of 2 or 3 males and a single female. The female deposit the eggs on a hard substratum. The spawning procedure lasts for a few weeks. The parents are to be removed as soon as it is over and the water level reduced to 2 cm as soon as the eggs begin to hatch. In some cases, the eggs can be detached from the substratum and affixed to the side panes of the glass aquarium, applying slight pressure. The eggs may be treated with Sodium chloride or Methylene blue in order to reduce mortality of eggs. The eggs hatch in four days and the young ones grow very fast. The fry can be fed with brine shrimp larvae.

4.1.31. Indian Glass Fish *(Chanda ranga)* (Fig. 51)

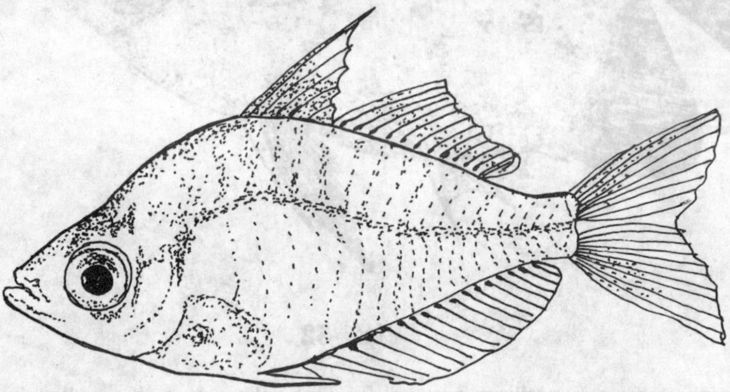

Fig. 51

This transparent fish is the native of India and Burma. The body is deep and short, growing to a size of 8 cm. Glass fish is exclusively carnivorous, feeding on only moving organisms, particularly zooplankton (water flea).

Aquarium breeding of this fish is possible, but rearing of young ones is relatively difficult. The male is more colourful than the female. The eggs are glassy and tiny. They hatch in 24 hours. The fry are to be fed with Infusoria and brine shrimp larvae.

4.1.32. Leopard Scat *(Scatophagus argus)*

It is a flat and deep bodied fish with dark brown to black spots on a metallic bronze green body. The fish can be fed on aquatic plants (duckweed), boiled egg, oat or corn flakes, etc. It grows to 30 cm in size.

The fish prefers slightly saline water (add a pinch of common salt to aquarium water) (Fig. 52).

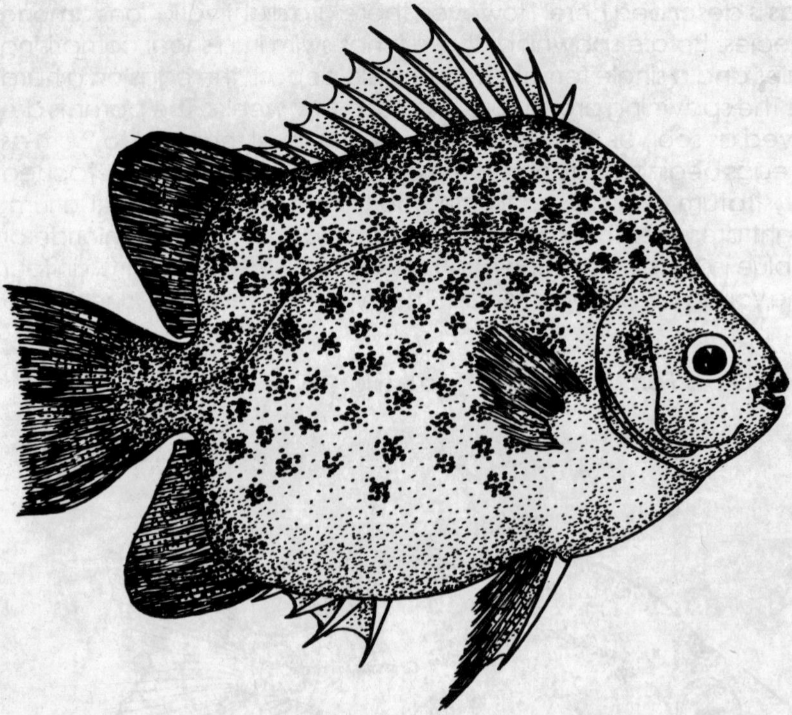

Fig. 52

Information regarding aquarium breeding is not available. They are peaceful school fish and can be trusted even with the smallest of fishes.

4.1.33.Oscar Cichlid *(Astronotus ocellatus)*

This strange cichlid which is a native of South America, is olive green in colour with a few fiery red markings on the body. It grows to 30 cm in size. Their food include small fishes, tadpoles, worms and insects. But they will thrive well on prepared foods also (Fig. 53).

The Oscars should be allowed to select their own mate. For this purpose, 10 to 12 fishes are to be reared together. As soon as they become mature, they select their own mate. A pair can be distinguished by its habit of cleaning rocks together and chasing other fishes in the aquarium. It is not easy to differentiate the sexes. Oscars spawn on smooth round rocks. Hence the aquarium tank should have rocks in the bottom. The eggs hatch in 3 days and the fry are moved to a pit nearby, prepared by the parents. Some Oscars tend to consume their own eggs. In such cases, it is always best to

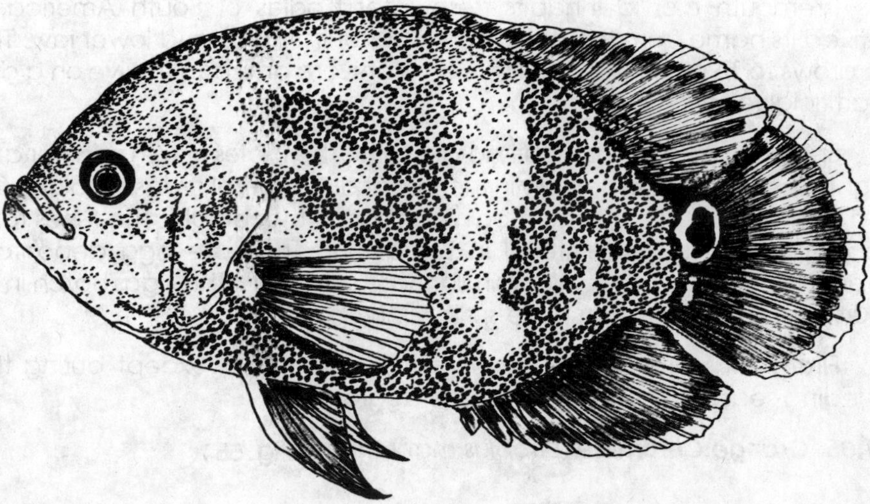

Fig. 53

transfer the eggs using a hose into an aquarium with similar water conditions. Few drops of Methylene blue should be added apart from providing profuse aeration. The fry starts exogenous nutrition in four to five days. They should then be fed on a diet of brine shrimp larvae . As they grow up, they can be fed on chopped tubifex worms. The juveniles are quite different from adults in appearance. The body is dark brown to black in colour with numerous patches on it.

4.1.34. Firemouth Cichlid *(Cichlasoma meeki)*

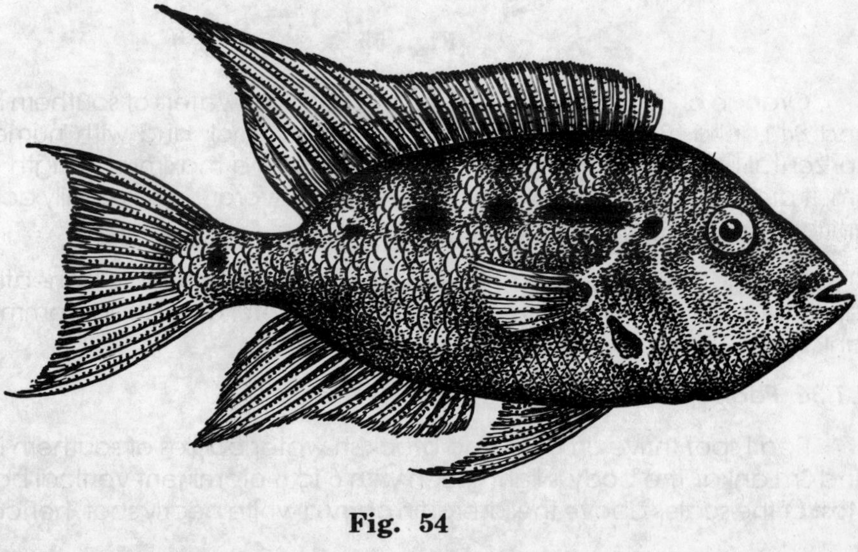

Fig. 54

Firemouth cichlid inhabits freshwater bodies of South America. It derived its name from the brick red colour of its throat and lower jaw. The fish grows to 15 cm in size. The fish is an omnivore and can survive on a diet of artificial feed (Fig. 54).

Spawning requires a slightly larger tank. The males have a darker and brighter colouration especially in the throat and ventral areas. Also, the fins and fin rays of males are more pointed than in the female. The fishes form stable pairs and are territorial in behaviour. They are egg depositors, depositing the eggs on rocks or similar hard substrata. The eggs hatch in 48 hours and the fry feed on brine shrimp larvae.

Firemouths are peaceful community tank fishes except during the breeding season when they become aggressive.

4.1.35. Orange Chromide *(Etroplus maculatus)* (Fig. 55)

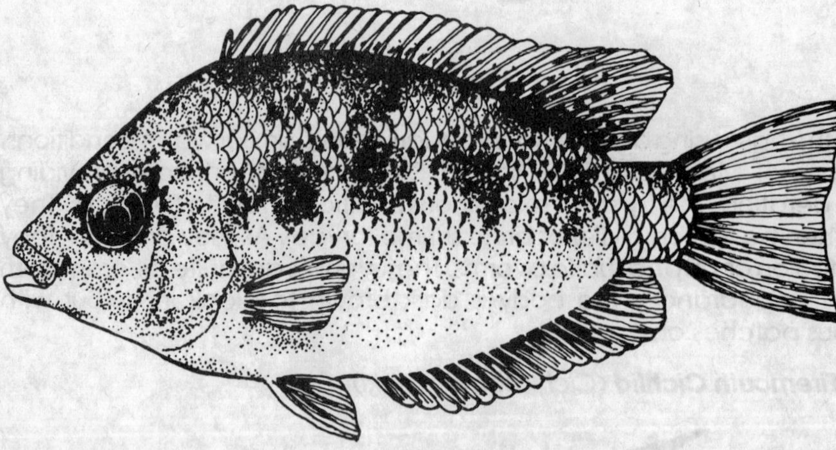

Fig. 55

Orange chromide inhabits fresh and brackish waters of southern India and Sri Lanka. Body is yellowish with greenish back and with numerous horizontal lines of orange golden spots. It attains a maximum length of 10 cm. It prefers slightly saline water. They are omnivorous and readily accept artificial food.

Orange chromides are very sensitive. They prefer to hide beneath the sand or gravel when agitated. They are peaceful and good community tank fishes.

4.1.36. Pearl Spot *(Etroplus suratensis)*

Pearl spot thrives in fresh and brackish water bodies of southern India and Sri Lanka. The body is light green with 6 to 8 prominent vertical bands. Most of the scales above the lateral fin carry a white pearly spot, hence the name 'Pearl Spot'. Pearl spot attains a maximum length of 40 cm. They require slightly saline waters. They thrive well in tanks with luxuriant growth of vegetation. Pearl spots are omnivorous, but show preference to soft leaved plants (Fig. 56).

Fig. 56

Sex differentiation is rather difficult. Males with more pointed anal fin. During breeding season, the adults dig small pits in sand using pectoral fins. Both the parents guard the eggs till they hatch.

They are peaceful and hence are very good community tank fishes. Pearl spot move in schools. Provide them plenty of soft leaved plants like *Elodea* as food.

4.1.37. Angel Fish *(Pterophyllum spp.)*

No aquarium is complete without Angel fishes. These deep bodied fishes are inhabitants of the Amazon basin. Altogether three species of Angel fishes are bred in the aquarium. *(Pterophyllum scalare, P. eimekei* and *P. altum*) Out of the three, *P. scalare* is the most popular. In addition to the original silver grey colour, several colours have been developed by the aquarium experts. These include the Zebra, black, marbled and golden angels. They reach a maximum of 15 cm. Their food comprises of both animal and plant matter. In captivity, canned meat products, mosquito larvae and tubifex worms are accepted apart from a diet of prepared aquarium food. It is always better to change the menu and provide them live feed in between (Fig. 57).

Fig. 57

A deep, thickly planted aquarium with lots of swimming space is required for breeding Angel fishes. It is difficult to distinguish the sex. Usually the about to spawn female has a larger belly, than the male. The genital papilla is pointed in the male and rounded in the female. In a school of Angels, if two fishes pair up and constantly give each other company, there is a good chance that they are a pair. They can be separated from the school and kept in a separate tank. Angels need smooth rocky substratum or broad leaved aquarium plants to deposit their eggs. In the spawning tank, provide broad leaved plants like *Echinodorus* (Amazon sword leaf plant) for the breeding purpose. Contrary to this, we have experienced the Angels depositing their eggs on the stem of water lillies even when Amazon plant and slate were provided.

Both adults show parental care. In case you suspect that the adults are egg eaters, transfer the eggs along with the spawning substratum to a separate tank containing a mild solution of methylene blue. Aeration should be given close to the eggs in order to provide water circulation. The eggs hatch in two days and the fry cling on to the leaf edges in clusters. In a week they are ready to accept brine shrimp larvae. Some adult fishes show parental care for a prolonged period. The parents are very aggressive during this period. The fry grow very fast and attain adult shape in four weeks.

Angel fishes are generally very peaceful when kept with fishes of their size or larger to them.

4.1.38. Discus *(Symphysodon spp.)* (Fig. 58)

Discus fish comes from the Amazon basin. Two species of Discus have been identified, *Sympysodon discus* (Real Discus) and *S. aequifasciatus* (Blue/ Brown Discus). Among them, the most beautiful and easily aquarium bred form is the Brown Discus. The body is flat and round, the shape of a disc. It grows to 20 cm in size. Their favourite food include blood worms, tubifex worms and mosquito larvae. But they can easily be supplemented with chopped beef meat or liver and dry artificial food.

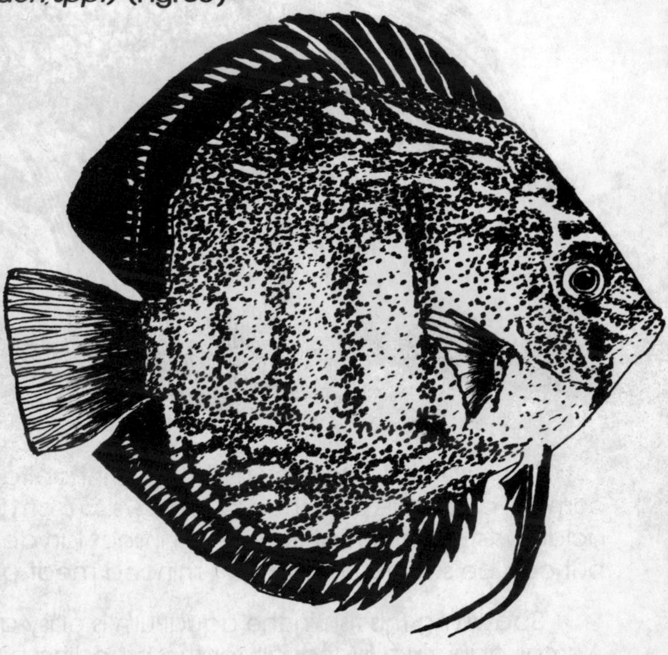

Fig. 58

Aquarium breeding is easy, but requires a large, deep and well planted tank. It is hard to distinguish the sex. Hence keep a school of fishes from which they select their own mate. The eggs are deposited on a smooth slanting substratum like a piece of slate or tile. The eggs hatch in 60 hours time and the newly hatched fry cling on to the substratum by short threads. The fry become free swimming in 4 to 5 days and attach themselves to the body of both the parents. The fry are nourished by the mucous secretion from the skin of the parents. The free swimming fry are to be fed on a steady supply of brine shrimp larvae.

Discus fishes are sensitive and require a large aquaria. They are extremely peaceful and can be kept in a community tank with other small fishes.

4.1.39. Siamese Fighting Fish (Betta splendens)

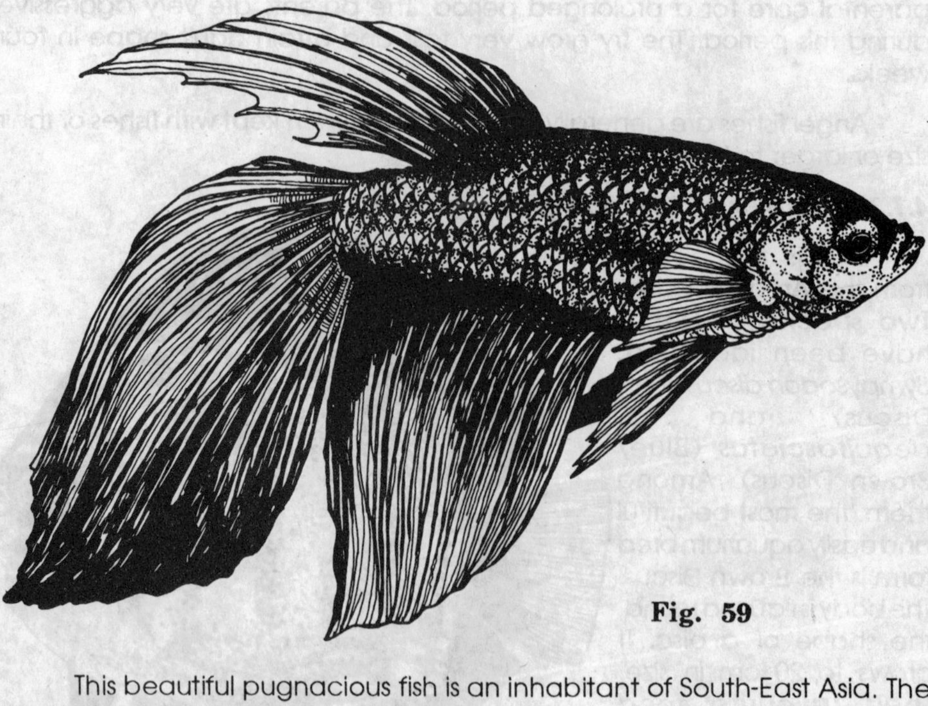

Fig. 59

This beautiful pugnacious fish is an inhabitant of South-East Asia. They come in all colours and shades. It grows to 6 cm in length. Bettas prefer soft acidic water. They mainly feed on insect larvae under natural conditions, but can be supplemented with minced meat and dried artificial food.

Spawning this fish in the aquarium is easy and require very little care. A small aquarium is enough for the breeding purpose. The spawners one year in age should be selected. Males have elongated fins and are much colourful than the females. The male builds a bubble nest beneath a floating leaf or on the sides of the aquarium. Some atmospheric air is taken into its mouth and enveloped using his saliva. These floating air globules are kept together to build the nest (avoid using aeration in the breeding tank to avoid damage of the bubble nest) (Fig. 59).

As soon as the female starts releasing her eggs, the male fertilizes them and collects the eggs in his mouth. These eggs are placed in the bubble nest by the male, often, assisted by the female. Remove the female as soon as spawning is over and males, as soon as the fry become free. The eggs hatch in 24 to 30 hours and the young ones should be fed with infusoria and later on with brine shrimp larvae. The water level should be lowered to around 2 cm. As soon as sex is able to be distinguished, separate the males and place them in individual jars, one next to the other. The females can be kept together in one tank.

Betta is a good community tank fish. But, care must be taken not to include two male Bettas, since they are bound to fight each other. It does not harm larger fishes but may consume smaller fishes like the larvae of live bearers.

4.1.40. Dwarf Gourami *(Colisa lalia)*

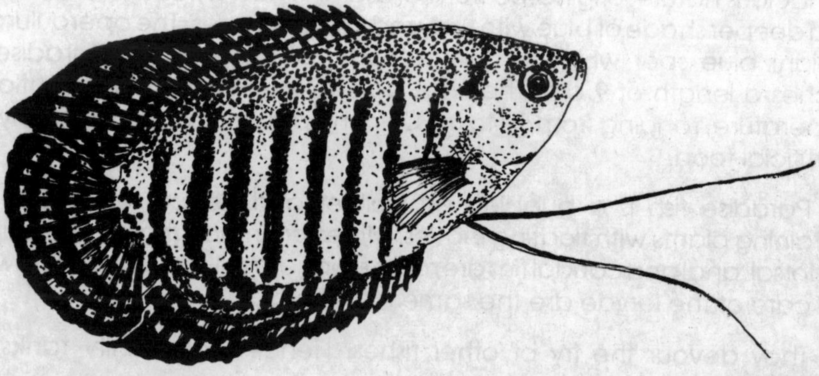

Fig. 60

These are one of the smallest but among the most beautiful of the Gouramies. It has its origin in North Eastern India. The body has a colour pattern of alternating metallic red and bluish green bands sloping across the flanks extending to the dorsal and anal fins. It reaches a size of 6 cm. The fish can thrive on both live as well as artificial food (Fig. 60).

Breeding these fishes is similar to that of fighting fish. The eggs hatch in a day and the fry are to be provided infusoria as diet. It is very difficult to rear the fry of Dwarf Gourami to adulthood.

The Dwarf Gourami is a very peaceful fish. But they are often very shy, hiding behind plant thickets. The aquarium should be heavily planted and well illuminated (preferably by sunlight). Keep the aquarium well covered to prevent them from jumping out.

***4.1.41. Paradise Fish** (Macropodus opercularis)* (Fig. 61).

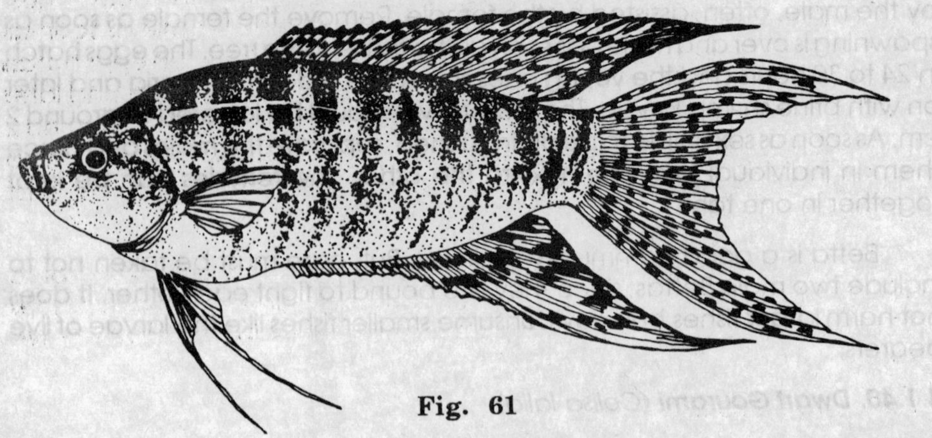

Fig. 61

This beautiful and interesting fish, often stunned by aquarists due to its pugnacious nature, originated from China and nearby countries. The body has a deeper shade of blue with rusty red vertical stripes. The operculum has a bright blue spot which is characteristic of this species. Paradise fish reaches a length of 9 cm. They are able to tolerate wide fluctuations in temperature, ranging from 10 to 32°C. In the aquarium it accepts any kind of artificial food.

Paradise fish is a bubble nest builder and hence requires a tank containing plants with floating leaves. Males are much more colourful and the dorsal, anal and caudal fins are more elongated and pointed. Spawning and care of the larvae are the same as in *Betta*.

They devour the fry of other fishes. Hence, community tanks with Paradise fish should not have smaller fishes.

***4.1.42. Pearl Gourami** (Tichogaster leeri)*

Pearl Gourami, one of the relatively larger aquarium fishes, is the inhabitant of South-East Asia. The brownish body is suffused with mosaic pearly spots. The fish grows to 12 cm in size. Their food comprises of tubifex worms and insect larvae. They readily accept prepared food (Fig. 62).

Aquarium breeding of Pearl Gourami is possible, but requires a lot of patience. The fish takes considerable amount of time to get sexually mature. The male can be distinguished by a slimmer body and an elongated dorsal fin. Spawning usually takes place in late evening. Spawning and larval rearing procedures are similar to *Betta*. The female does not eat the eggs. But to be on the safer side remove them as soon as spawning is over and males as soon as the fry become free swimming. Hatching of eggs occur in a day's time. The young ones grow very slowly.

Pearl Gourami is a peaceful fish, not even aggressive during the spawning period.

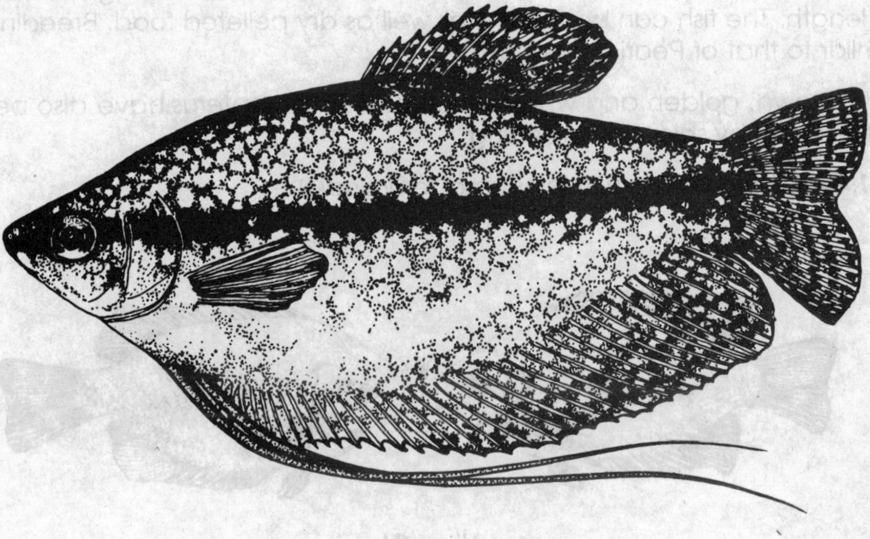

Fig. 62

4.4.43. Blue Gourami or Three Spot Gourami *(Trichogaster trichopterus)*

Fig. 63

Blue Gourami has its origin in the far east. The fish has a black spot on its caudal peduncle and another spot on the middle of the body. These two spots along with the black eye on a powder blue body is responsible for the name, the Three Spot Gourami. The Blue Gourami attains a length of 15 cm in length. The fish can be fed live as well as dry pelleted food. Breeding is similar to that of Pearl Gourami.

Brown, golden and white varieties of *T. trichopterus* have also been developed by selective breeding.

***4.1.44. Kissing Gourami** (Helostoma temmincki)*

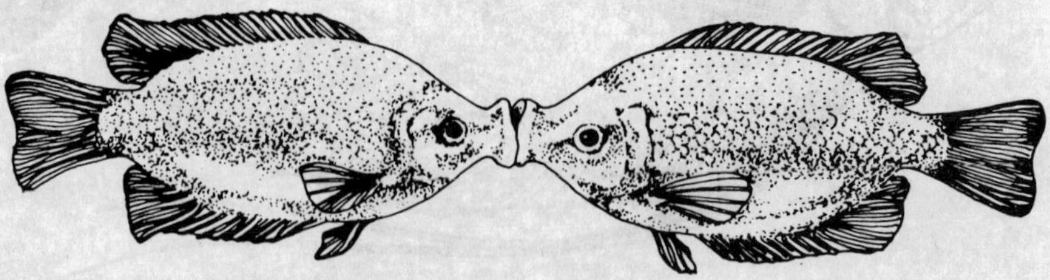

Fig. 64

This popular aquarium fish oiginated from Thailand and Malaya Archipelago. The fish derived its name from the behaviour of kissing lip to lip. Kissing gouramies grow to a size of 50 cm in length. The fish has thick protruding lips equipped with fine teeth suited for scraping algae from rocks. The fish is also reported to feed on nannoplankton, by seiving them with the help of their gills (Fig. 64).

The posterior end of the dorsal and anal fins are sharp cornered in males, while it is rounded in females. Apart from that there is no distinguishing character to separate the sexes. The males do not build bubble nests. Female lays 30-50 floating eggs. This process is repeated several times. It is advisable to remove the eggs promptly to water of similar chemical composition. The eggs hatch in 52 hours and start feeding in five days on Infusoria and brine shrimp larvae. Kissing gouramies are peaceful and highly valued due to its kissing behaviour, which is nothing but a harmless fight between two males during which one pushes the other with its thick lips.

4.2. Live Bearing Fishes

In members of this group, the fertilization is internal and the eggs hatch within her body. They give birth to fully developed young fishes. The males of live bearers can easily be distinguished by the presence of a gonopodium (modification of the fourth, fifth and sixth rays of the anal fin) which is the copulatory organ. The live bearers are prolific breeders; most of the time difficult to stop them from breeding.

***4.2.1. Guppy** (Poecilia reticulata)* (Fig. 65)

Fig. 65

Guppy, hailing from Central America is the most popular of all tropical aquarium fishes. Colour of both male and female fish vary greatly. Tail pattern of male fish also exhibit gross variations (see Fig. 66).

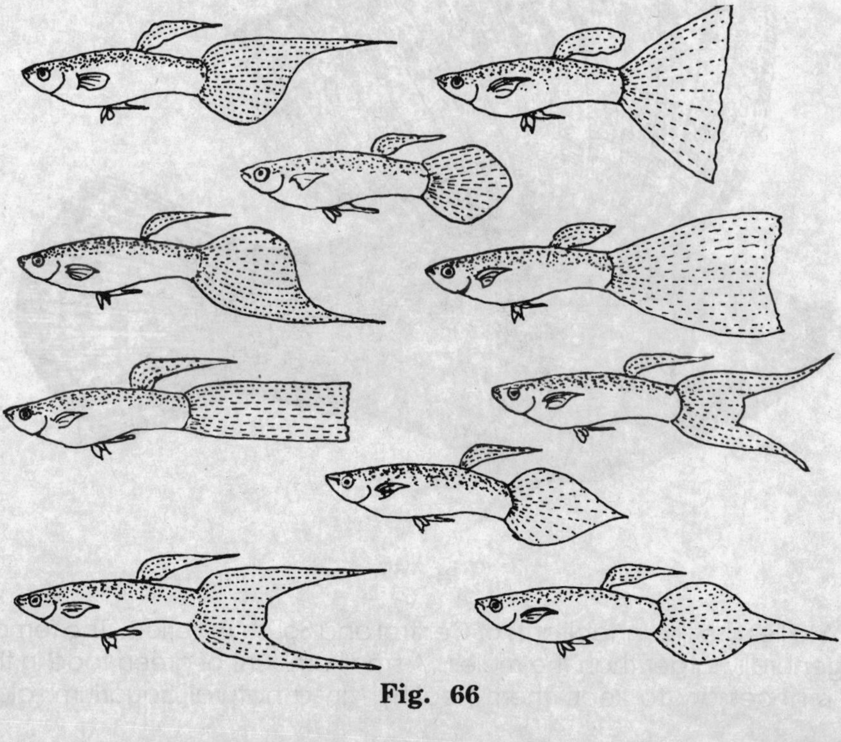

Fig. 66

The females grow to 5 cm in size, while the smaller males reach only around 3 cm. Guppy is omnivorous and can be reared on a diet of artificial feed.

They are prolific breeders and most often it is difficult to stop these fishes from breeding. The male possess a very flexible gonopodium which aids him in copulation. The fry come out of the mother with their tail first followed by the anterior part of the body. A small yolk sac will be present at the belly region. The fry starts feeding as soon as this is absorbed into the body. The fry can be fed with fine boiled egg yolk or dried water flea during this period. During this period the female should be kept in a separate well planted tank in case breeding trap is not available. Successive breedings occur at an interval of 4 to 6 weeks. Try to collect brood fish of the same strain from unrelated sources to reduce inbreeding.

Guppies are very hardy and often survive in poorly oxygenated waters and confined swimming spaces. They are very active fishes, always on the move. Keep them in large numbers.

4.2.2. Mollies *(Poecilia spp.)*

Fig. 67

Mollies are the inhabitants of Central and South America. The females are generally larger than the males. A small amount of green food in their diet is necessary to keep them healthy. In a natural aquarium, algae attached to plants, glass panes and rocks form part of their food. Care must be taken to remove the left over food before decay occurs. Tubifex worms and artificial food can also be provided to the Mollies. The commonly available Molly species include *Poecilia velifera* or the Sail Fin Molly (Fig. 67) and *Poecilia sphenops* or the Black Molly. (Fig. 68)

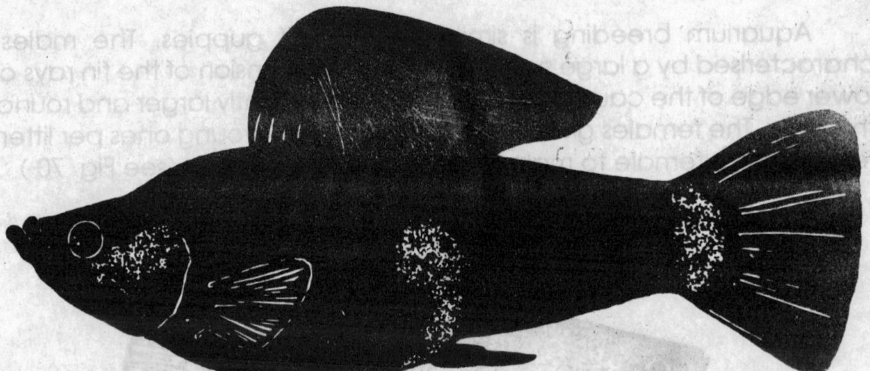

Fig. 68

Breeding is similar to that in Guppies, but care should be taken not to disturb fully pregnant females, because this results in premature release of the fry.

4.2.3 Sword Tail *(Xiphophorus helleri)*

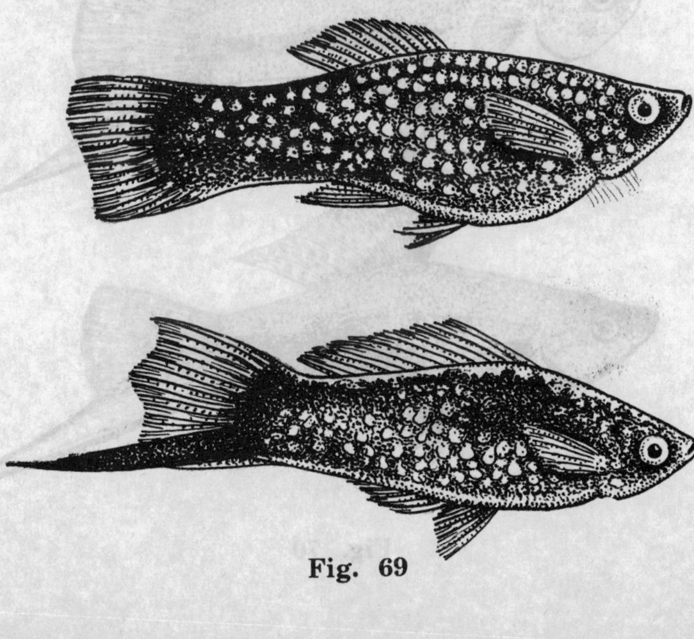

Fig. 69

Sword tail is the inhabitant of Central America. The wild form is a stream lined fish, olive green in colour with males having short swords. A whole range of colour strains were developed later through selective breeding. The sword tails prefer vegetable matter in their diet. If algae is scarce in your aquarium, provide boiled lettuce, cabbage or spinach as supplementary feed (Fig. 69).

Aquarium breeding is similar to that of guppies. The males are characterised by a large sword which is the extension of the fin rays of the lower edge of the caudal fin. The females are slightly larger and rounder in the belly. The females give birth to as high as 200 young ones per litter. Sex reversal from female to male is common in this species (see Fig. 70)

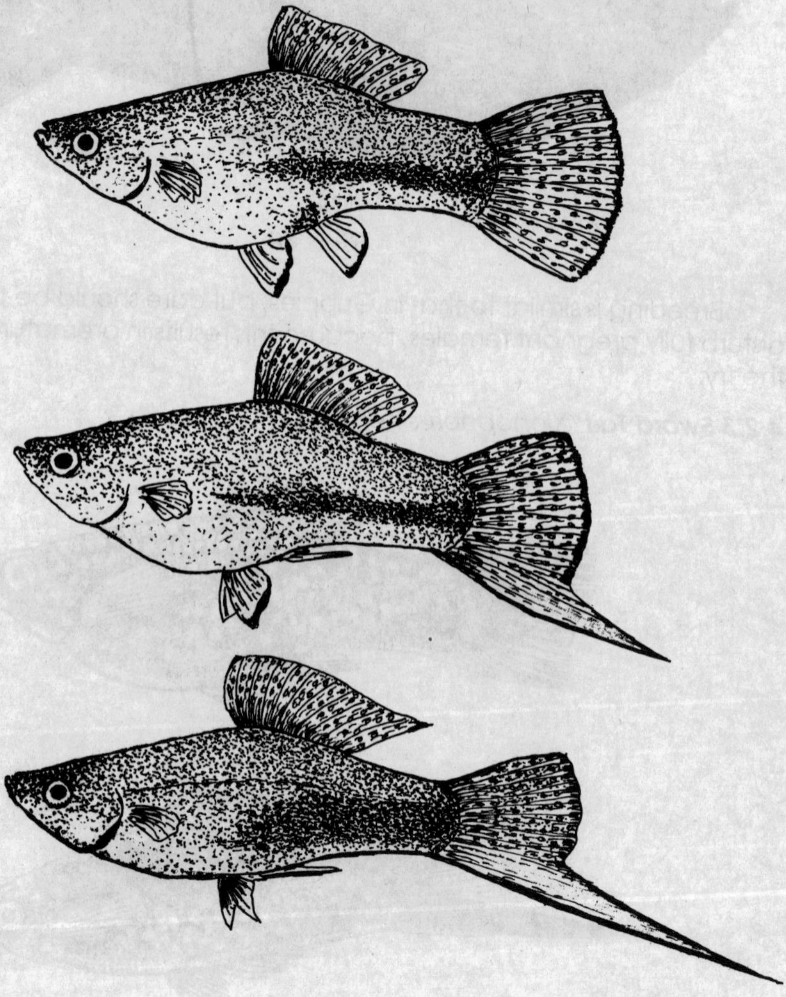

Fig. 70

Always keep them with fishes larger or equal in size to them, since they attack smaller fishes. Keep the aquarium properly covered as Sword Tails are accomplished jumpers.

The different varieties of Sword Tails are green, red, white, wag tail, tuxedo and simpson.

4.2.4. Platy *(Xiphophorus spp.)*

Platy hails from Central America. The body of Platies are slightly shorter and deeper than that of Sword Tails. Males are smaller and grow to a size of 3 cm, while the females reach 5 cm in size. They are available in a whole range of shades. Green algae from a major part of their food.

Like all live bearers, aquarium breeding is very easy. A breeding trap may be used since they consume the fry. The gonopodium in the males and fuller belly in the females are the distinguishing features for determining the sex. The number of fry in a single brood amount to 100. They often cross breed with the Sword Tails. The platies are very active and well behaved, aptly suited for a community tank.

Xiphophorus maculatus and *X. variatus* are the two species of platies very common in the aquariums world over. *X. maculatus* is a species with varying colours even in the natural environment. Some of the common varieties of this species include:

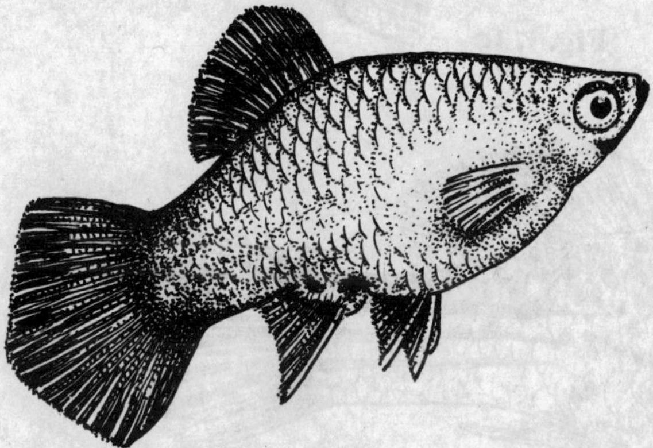

Fig. 71a

(i) Coral Platy: This is the most common red variety with whitish-blue tinge in the ventral, anal and caudal fins.

(ii) Wagtail Platy (Fig. 71a): Body colour of this species may be grey, yellow or red, with deep black fins.

(iiii) Simpson Platy (Fig. 71b): This long-established aquarium fish appearing in various shades has an elongated dorsal fin.

(iv) Spitz Platy (Fig. 71c): This variety is recognised by the possession of elongated fin flays in the middle part of the caudal fin. However, this form is not yet genetically fixed.

The Variegated Platy (X. Variatus) (Fig. 71d) shows patches of colours in the body, hence the name. The typical colour of this fish is drab olive, with

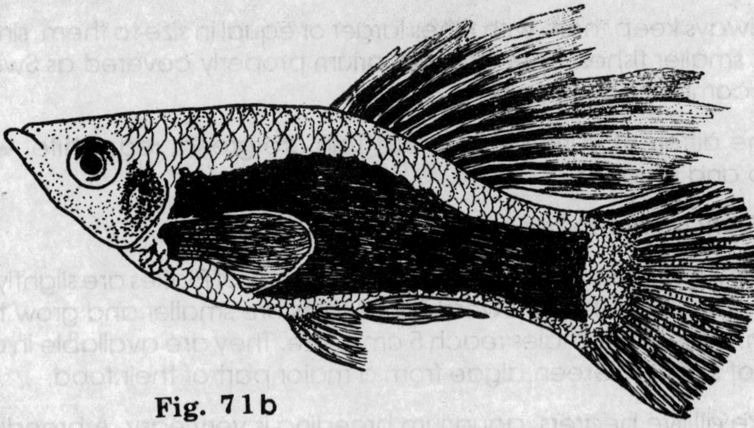

Fig. 71b

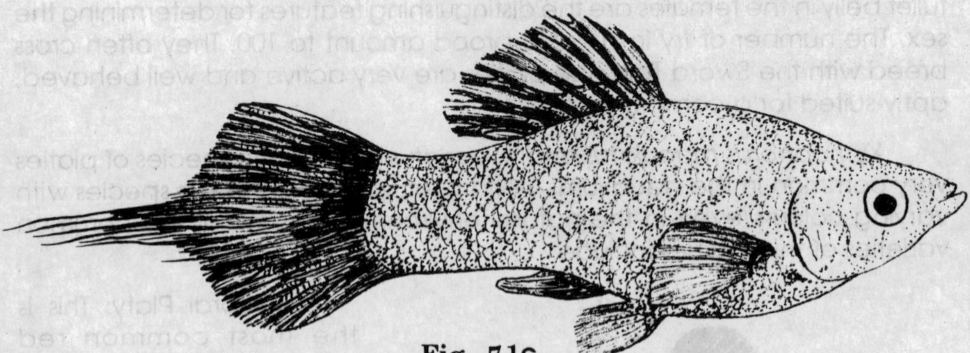

Fig. 71c

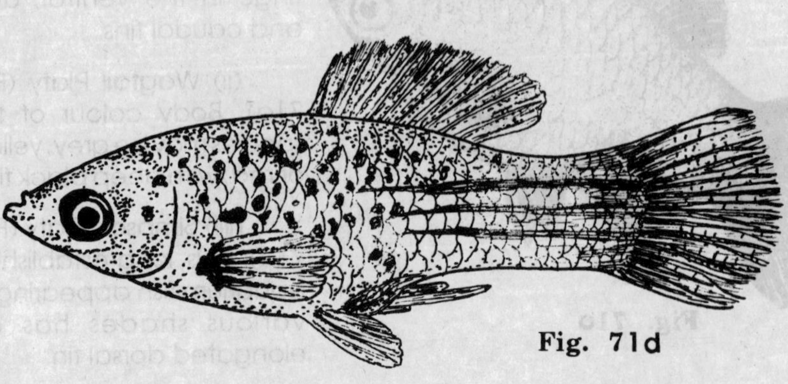

Fig. 71d

males showing considerable colour variations. Males bear a dark spot on the flanks (above the vent), resembling the pregnancymark in femals. Body of Variegated Platy is more sleeker and is a prolific breeder compared to *X. maculatus.* These two species interbreed very often and it is rather difficult to distinguish the species now. Variegated Platy appears in many colour forms like albinotic, red, tuxedo, gold wagtail, marigold black, etc.

BREEDING

Breeding aquarium fishes require a good amount of care and patience. There is a remarkable difference in the techniques involved in breeding the egg layers and live bearers. Breeding fish in the aquarium comprises of the following steps:

1. Setting up the spawning tank
2. Selection of spawners
3. Conditioning the brood fishes
4. Spawning
5. Rearing the fry

Each fish has its own specifications regarding physico-chemical and environmental factors related to spawning. In the spawning tank always try to provide an environment similar to one in its natural habitat. Care must be taken to control the temperature, pH, hardness, water column level,etc., according to the requirement of individual fish. Unless proper care is taken, the eggs or the fry have very little chance of surviving. Spawning grids or traps may be used in the breeding tank in order to save the eggs from being eaten by the parents. The place where the aquarium is kept is also important since some fishes like the Dwarf Gourami need sunlight, while others like the Neon or Cardinal Tetras prefer a dark aquarium. Even the development of the embryos of Neon and Cardinal Tetras are affected by harsh sunlight. But, the general rule is to cut down the illumination to its minimum in case the breeding fish is an egg eater. Temperature also plays a very important role in spawning. A few degrees rise or fall in temperature may change a listless fish into a glowing one anxious to breed. Most of the Tetras prefer soft acidic water while the live bearers are totally the opposite, preferring hard alkaline water. The choice of the breeding tank is also very important. Even if the fish is small and requires very little space, the rule is to use as large an aquarium as possible for the breeding purpose. In a large tank, fluctuation or variation in temperature caused by the heater is less affected than in a small tank. The aquarium may be thickly planted in order to prevent the fish from exploring for eggs after spawning is over.

The next step regarding spawning of aquarium fishes is the selection of spawners. Always select fishes that are healthy, having the required/ desired qualities or those equalling aquarium standards. Similarly eliminate diseased fishes and those with visible anatomical or genetic deformities like tumours, deformed spinal cord, etc. To get best results, employ selective breeding (see Glossary).

Select spawners from different sources to minimise inbreeding. In the case of live-bearers, the only way to avoid inbreeding is to separate the males from females, once the sex could be distinguished.

Fig. 72

Most of the spawners have to be conditioned before spawning. The male and female fishes are reared separately for one or two weeks (Fig. 72). During this period, the fish are fed on live food available in its natural environment. Fishes like the barbs and tetras are usually conditioned on a diet of live food like mosquito larvae, tubifex worms etc. Some aquarists often provide a menu with varying diets of live food each day. Not all egg layers are to be conditioned separately. Some fishes like the Angel and Oscar need to be kept together in a shoal or pair for a long time before breeding takes place. In such cases the school may be fed on a varying diet of live food. They are not to be separated once they pair up for spawning. Considering live-bearers, conditioning is not always necessary.

The conditioned fishes are usually relased into the breeding tank at dusk. In some cases, the females are released atleast a day or two prior to the release of the male. This is to familiarise the female with the aquarium conditions and to minimise fear. Fishes are to be released in a school or in pairs depending on their spawning behaviour. Fishes like the Danios are to be released in schools with larger number of males.

Rearing the fry is the most difficult part. If the eggs and fry are not given proper care, all your effort will be in vain. The eggs are to be tendered properly preventing them from any fungal attack. A few drops of Methylene blue into the tank will minimise the fungal attack. The eggs infected by the fungus are to be removed as soon as possible. This is to reduce further fungal attack. There is nothing more difficult than finding the right food for the new born fishes.

The dietary requirements of the fries of different aquarium fishes are given in Table II. An account of the culture of various live food organisms have also been provided in Chapter 3.

Breeding techniques and devices involved in breeding differ according to spawning behaviour of the fish. The spawning behaviour differs with each family. Variation are also present among members of the same family. The egg layers can be classified into different categories depending on their breeding habits.

1. Egg scatterers
2. Egg depositors
3. Mouth brooders
4. Bubble nest builders

5.1. Egg Scatterers

Eg:- Danios, gold fish, hatchet fish, glass fish, kissing gouramies, Tetras, flying barb, Barbs, *Rasbora*, etc.

The egg scatterers release eggs in a haphazard manner, scattering the eggs in all directions. Once the spawning is over, they often consume the eggs. The egg scatterers show no parental care. Hence it is the job of the aquarist to protect the eggs from being eaten by the parents. A thickly planted aquarium with less swimming space may be used for eggs which are adhesive in nature (eg. eggs of gold fish). This often helps the eggs from being eaten. In the case of non-adhesive eggs (eg. eggs of danios), an aquarium with low water column and a bottom laid with pebbles or marbles may be used. The egg scatterers usually show less interest in the eggs while the spawning is in progress. They start feeding on eggs only after spawning is over.

Breeding traps and grids may be installed for better survival rate of the eggs. For eggs scatterers, spawning grids are to be placed with mesh size relative to the size of the egg. Usually mesh size of 3x3 mm to 6x6 mm are used. The grids can be constructed in two ways. A net with required mesh size may be attached to the upper side of a 5 cm thick plastic frame with frame size corresponding to the inner dimensions of the aquarium. The frame should be lowered to the bottom of the tank so that a water column of 5 cm exists between the net and the bottom of the tank. (Fig. 73).Precaution must be taken not to leave space between the sides of the tank and the plastic frame, for the fish to enter. Another method is to

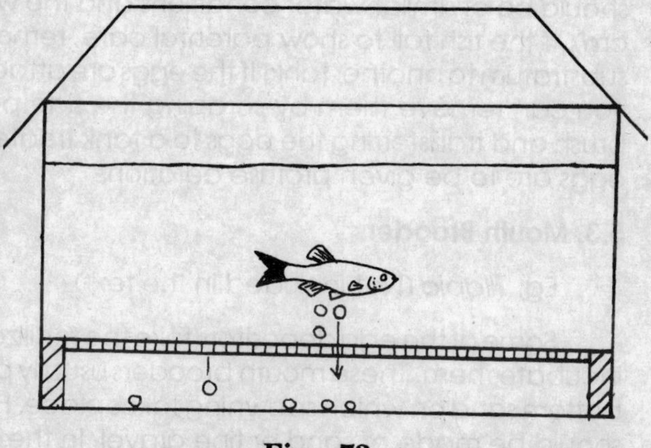

Fig. 73

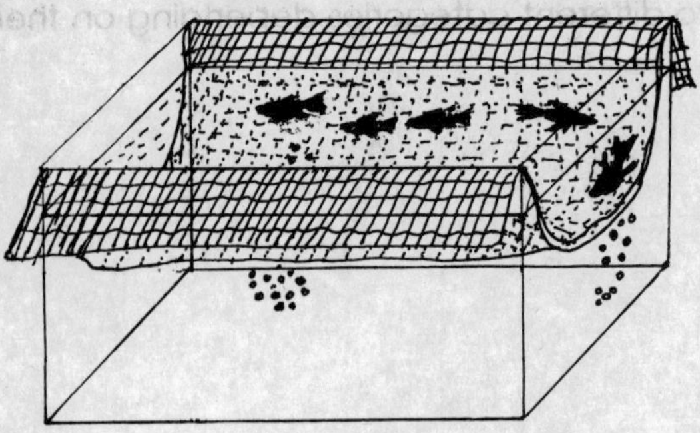

Fig. 74

place a piece of net (with required mesh size) across the aquarium with the central portion immersed below the surface providing sufficient swimming space (Fig. 74). Care must be taken not to provide escape routes while placing the net. In both cases, the eggs fall through the net and are collected at the bottom of the tank.

5.2. Egg Depositors

Eg:- Chichlids like Discus and Angel fish, Firemouth cichlid, Oscar cichlid, etc.

The egg depositors care more for their young than egg-hangers or scatterers. These are mostly cichlids which show parental care. They need substratum like leaves, rocks, flower pots, tiles or slates to deposit the eggs. Hence the spawning tank should contain hard substratum like rocks, slanting slates or tiles etc., which can be easily removed. Most of the depositors select their own pair/mate. It is best to remove the fry once they become free swimming, even though the fish shows parental care. The tank should be of similar water conditions and the water column very low (5-10 cm). If the fish fail to show parental care, remove the eggs along with the substratum to another tank. If the eggs are attached to the sides of the tank, you can remove them by scraping the side panes or by means of a fine brush and transferring the eggs to a tank treated with methylene blue. The eggs are to be given profuse aeration.

5.3. Mouth Brooders

Eg: *Tilapia* (Not included in the text)

Some of the egg depositors take the fertilized eggs into their mouth and incubate them. These mouth brooders usually prepare breeding pits on the bottom sand on which spawning takes place. Hence the aquarium bottom should be made of sand or fine gravel. In the case of Tilapias, the female carries the eggs in her mouth. The eggs hatch inside the mouth and the parent carry the fry also for some time. Some of the mouth brooders tend to gulp the eggs. This may be due to numerous factors like young and inexperienced spawners, insufficient room or unfavourable conditions. Some female mouth brooders carry the eggs/ fry in their mouth for some time and then swallow them. This can be prevented by trapping the female in a fine net without disturbing the fish much. Then the fish is to be held in the hand with the head immersed in a small bowl. Slowly open the mouth by applying pressure on to the lower jaw with your index finger. Then shake the fish gently in water. Soon the eggs/fry are released into the bowl. These eggs/fry are to be transferred to an aquarium with very little water column and given profuse aeration.

5.4.Nest Builders

Eg: - *Betta*, gouramies, paradise fish, etc.

Some fishes build bubble nests during the time of breeding, The bubble nest is usually built under a floating leaf or on the sides of the aquarium. The bubble nest is made of fine air bubbles coated with saliva. Aerating the aquarium should be avoided since this results in the destruction of the bubble nest. The male guard the eggs once the spawning is over. In some cases, the female also aids him in this process. The female should be removed as soon as spawning is over, while the male should be removed as soon as the fry become free swimming.

5.5.Live-bearing Fishes

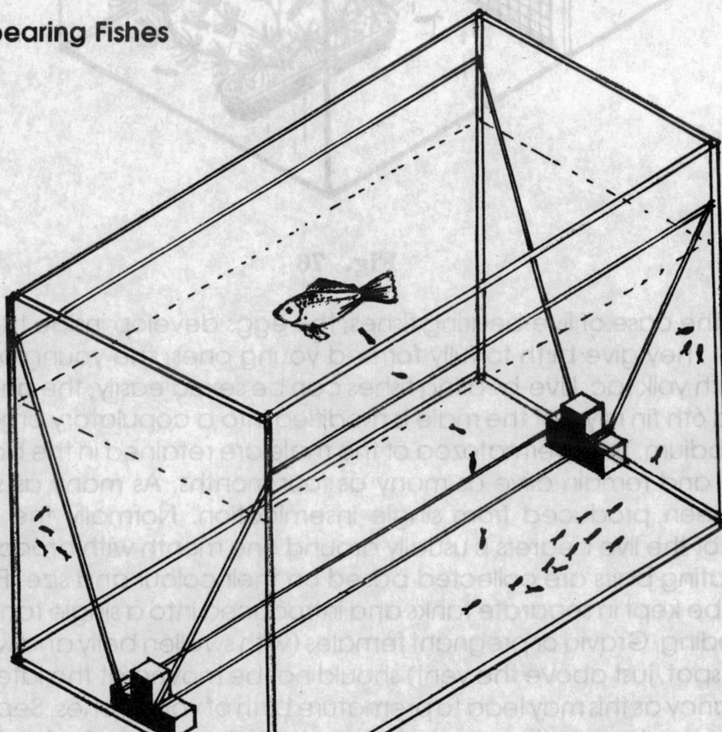

Fig. 75

Fig. 76

In the case of live-bearing fishes, the eggs develop inside the body of mother. They give birth to fully formed young ones; the young ones often born with yolk sac. Live-bearing fishes can be sexed easily, the anal fin (4th, 5th and 6th fin rays) of the male is modified into a copulatory organ called gonopodium. The spermatozoa of the male are retained in the body of the female and remain alive as many as four months. As many as six broods have been produced from single insemination. Normally the gestation period of the live bearers is usually around one month with brood from 5 to 250. Mating pairs are collected based on their colour and size. Both sexes should be kept in separate tanks and introduced into a single tank just prior to breeding. Gravid or pregnant females (with swollen belly and with a dark gravid spot, just above the vent) should not be moved at the later stage of pregnancy as this may lead to premature birth of young ones. Separate the gravid females into the spawning tank. Well planted tank with diffuse illumination is most suitable for breeding live bearers. Remove the female as soon as the young are born. Breeding traps (Figs.75 & 76) may be used to prevent the female fish from devouring her young fry.

DISEASES

Both in home aquaria and in intensive ornamental fish culture, disease is one of the serious limiting factors impeding the growth of fishes and causing heavy mortalities. In most parts of the world, particularly in Asian countries, where ornamental fish trade is a flourishing business, disease has become a serious menace, severely affecting the ornamental fish trade industry. Losses of 50-100 % of the consignments for the export of ornamental fishes have been reported every year due to diseases of some kind or the other. Since the potential for the development of ornamental fish industry is vast in India, the role of disease affecting ornamental fishes should be better realised and given due recognition. In short, control of diseases is a vital aspect in maintaining a healthy aquarium and for the successful mass production of ornamental fishes.

Diseases can generally be classified into communicable diseases (caused by microbes and parasites), non-communicable diseases (caused by environmental, nutritional and genetic factors and certain conditions of unknown causes) and neoplastic diseases (tumours and cancers).

6.1. Bacterial Diseases

6.1.1. Cloud Eye

This disease is very common in Gold Fish, Barbs, Angel Fishes, Mollies and Sword Tails. Though diseases like Oodiniasis, Tuberculosis etc. may also cause cloud eye, non-specific bacterial infections are believed to be responsible for this disease. Due to this disease, either one or both the eyes become cloudy-white (opaque). It can be treated based on the pathogens involved. However, by observing total cleanliness, occurrence of this disease can be minimised.

6.1.2. Columnaris or Cotton-Wool Disease

It is a common bacterial disease of live bearing aquarium fishes, caused by *Flexibacter (Chondrococcus) columnaris.* Wrongly called 'Mouth Fungus', this disease makes its appearance as greyish white spots on the skin, particularly around the mouth. At the advanced stages, the body becomes ulcerated. Fishes with severe mouth infection may die within 24 hours. This disease can be treated by dipping the fishes in 1: 2000 Copper sulphate solution (1 part $CuSO_4$: 2000 part water) for one to two minutes or in 1 : 15, 000 Malachite green for 10 to 30 seconds. For treatment of ponds, addition of 1 mg of $CuSO_4$/litre has been recommended.

6.1.3. Dropsy or Hydrops or Ascites

Caused by *Aeromonas (Pseudomonas)* bacteria, this disease is characterised by the accumulation of liquid inside the body cavity. Important signs of this disease include distended abdomen followed by ulcer formation, scale and eye protrution (exophthalmus or pop eye). This disease is common in carps and gouramies, particularly in dwarf gourami (*Colisa lalia*). Treating the infected fishes with antibiotics like Chloromycetin (13 mg/litre of water) has been reported to be effective. No food should be given during treatment.

6.1.4. Fin Rot or Tail Rot

Fin Rot or Tail Rot is the most common bacterial disease in aquarium fishes. This disease is caused by different species of *Aeromonas* particularly *A. hydrophila.* The apparent symptom of this disease is progressive erosion of the caudal fin. Frequently a secondary fungal infection occurs. It is also found that poor environmental conditions accelerate the occurrence of this disease. Although surgical removal of diseased regions is necessary in advanced stages of infection, this disease during initial stages can be treated by Phenoxethol (2 mg/L for one hour), Chloromycetin (13 mg/L of water). 'Potasssium permanganate (10 ppm)' etc. Short baths for 1 to 2 minutes in 1: 2000 solution of copper sulphate till the fish shows signs of distress is also found to be useful in controlling tail rot.

6.1.5. Scale Protrution

In aquaria, one may come across a disease in which the scales of a fish project out at right angles to their body surface. This scale protrution disease occurring due to the oedema of the scale pocket is caused by the bacterium, *Bacterium lepidothosae.* This disease is commonly observed in Bettas. Though there is no effective treatment for this disease, Chloromycetin or Sulphanilamide (10 mg/L of water) could be tried.

6.1.6. Ulcer Disease

This disease starts as patches on the body and fins which later develops into open ulcers. This paves way to secondary invaders like fish fungus, *Saprolegnia.* The ulcers are caused mainly by *Aeromonas* and *Pseudomonas* bacteria. Since external application of antibiotics are not found to be sucessfull, antibiotics like chloromycetin and Oxytetracyclin added to the food at the rate of 50 mg/kg of fish/ day was found to be effective. Severely infected fish should be destroyed and the water should be disinfected with 0.5 ppm solution of Potassium permanganate.

6.2. Fungal Diseases

6.2.1. Fish Fungus

Fungi infesting a wide variety of aquarium fishes mainly belongs to the genera, *Achlya* and *Saprolegnia*. Fungi are mostly secondary invaders, infections occurring usually after mechanical injury or other kinds of damages to the skin. The signs of this disease are cotton wool like growth on fish or fish egg. It may spread to fins, mouth, eyes and gills. Heavy infection result in osmotic imbalance, respiratory impairment and finally death of the infected fish. Infected fish can be treated by short baths in 3% common salt (Sodium chloride) solution or 1:2000 solution of Copper sulphate or in 1:1000 solution of Potassium permanganate for 5 to 10 minutes or until the fish shows signs of distress. Formalin has been used mainly for treating infection of eggs.

6.3. Protozoan Diseases

6.3.1. 'Ich' or White Spot Disease

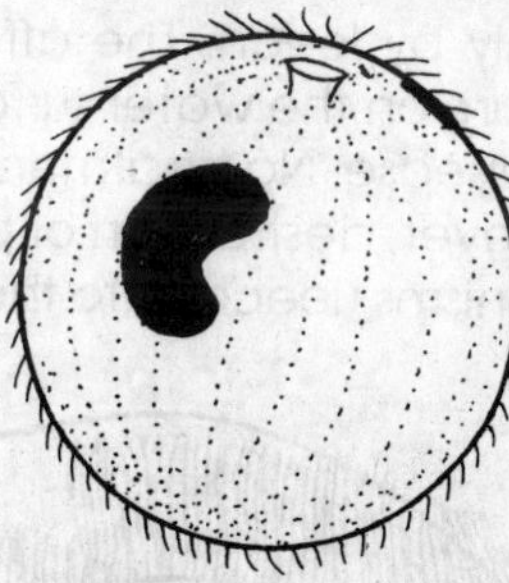

Fig. 77

This is the most common and well studied disease affecting all varieties of aquarium fishes. This disease is characterised by small white specks on the body surface and on the gills of affected fish. Each such spot represents the site of the encysted ciliate parasite. *Ichthyophthirius multifilis.* The infected fish rub their body against hard surfaces and try to jump out of water. Then they cease to feed, become discoloured, lethargic and finally die. Occurrence of this disease can be controlled by increasing the temperature to 32°C. However this was not found useful in most of the cases since majority of aquarium fishes die at this temperature. The recommended treatments are: short salt baths at 25,000 to 30,000 ppm for 10 to 15 minutes and short dip treatments in 0.5 ppm Malachite green and 3 ppm Methylene blue 3 to 6 times a day.

6.3.2. Neon Tetra Disease

This disease has been first observed in Neon Tetra and hence the name. It has also been reported from other aquarium fishes like carps, danios and minnows. The causative organism, *Pleistophora hyphessobryconis* form cysts in the intestine or muscle of the infected fish. These cysts destroy the muscle fibres gradually and are released when the skin is damaged and when the fish dies. No effective treatment has been found for this disease.

However, anti parasitic drugs could be tried for controlling this disease.

6.3.3. Nodular Disease

Myxobolus (Thelohanellus) and other protozoan parasites are responsible for this disease in aquarium fishes. Infected fish show small oval cysts on the gill and skin. This infection is most dangerous to the young fish and hene is advisable to seggregate different age group of fishes to reduce the chances of infection from older fish. The infected fish should be destroyed and the tank be disinfected since control measures are found to be ineffective (Fig. 78).

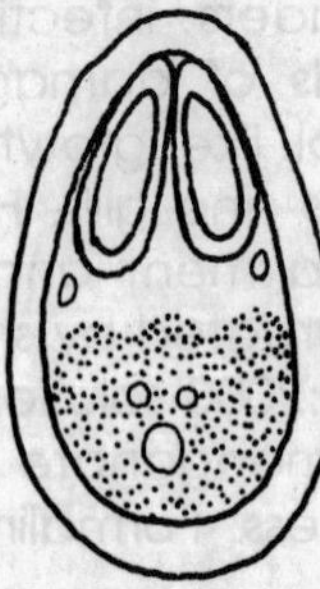

Fig. 78

6.3.4. Sleeping Sickness

Blood flagellate, *Trypanosoma* spp. is responsible for this disease. Blood flagellates are transmitted mainly by leech. The affected fish lie in a sleeping posture on the water surface with little movement and hence the name of the disease. No treatment has been developed for controlling this disease. However, destruction or prevention of the entry of the disease transmitting organisms (leech) into the aquarium is the only way to control this disease.

6.3.5. Trichodiniasis

Trichodina is most common in the ornamental fish farms of Asian countries, infecting a wide variety of ornamental fishes. They invade the skin and gill of the host, causing degeneration of the epithelial cells followed by excess mucous production. A dull light whitish coating of mucous develops on the affected surface. If the aquarium is overcrowded, Trichodines infecting fishes multiply rapidly resulting in mass mortalities of young fishes. Short baths in common salt solutions of different concentrations (2000 to 50,000 ppm) depending upon the intensity of infection is used effectively in controlling Trichodines (Fig. 79).

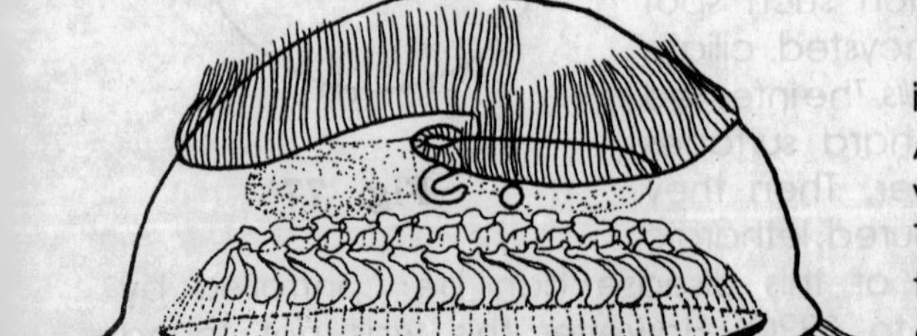

Fig. 79

6.3.6. Velvet Disease or Oodiniasis (Fig. 80).

Fishes suffering from this disease has a dusty appearance on the skin. The protozoan parasite *Oodinium* is responsible for this disease. It infests the skin and induces excess mucous production. Young fishes may succumb to infection within two weeks. The best way to prevent *Oodinium* infection is to disinfect water before filling the tank. Quarantine of newly purchased fishes for two weeks is also recommended. Short dips in common salt solution for 1 to 2 minutes at 35,000 ppm, 2-3 ppm Methylene blue treatment for 3 to 5 days and 1-2 ppm Copper sulphate bath for an indeterminate time has been recommended.

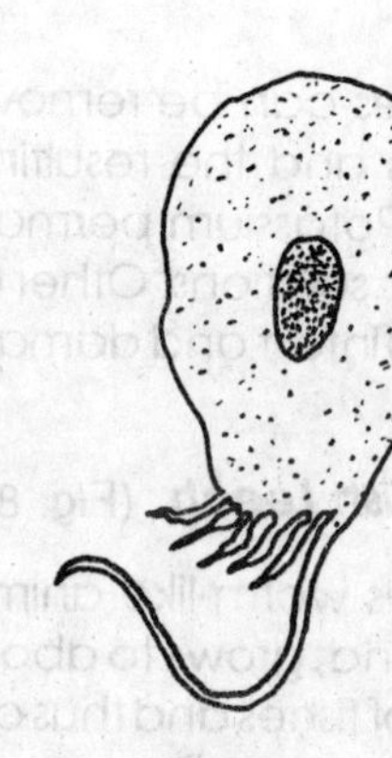

Fig. 80

6.4. Parasitic Diseases (Fig. 81).

6.4.1. Anchor Worm *(Lernaea spp.)*

Females of this copepod parasite has a long 'worm' like body (about 20 mm) with anchor like appendages at the head, which penetrates deep into the muscle and internal organs. The wounds produced by this parasite may pave way to secondary infection by bacteria or fungi. Individual

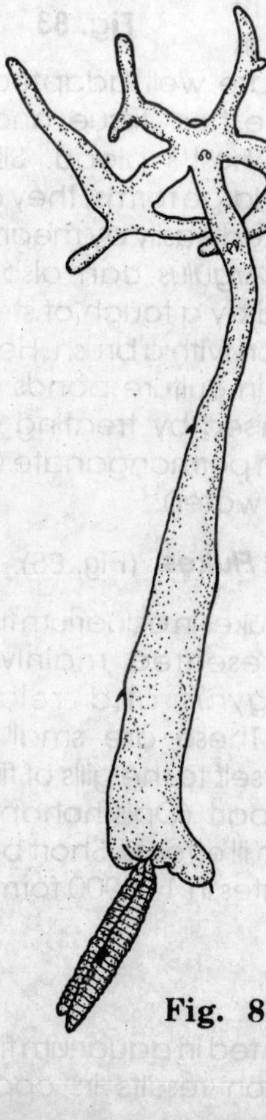

Fig. 81

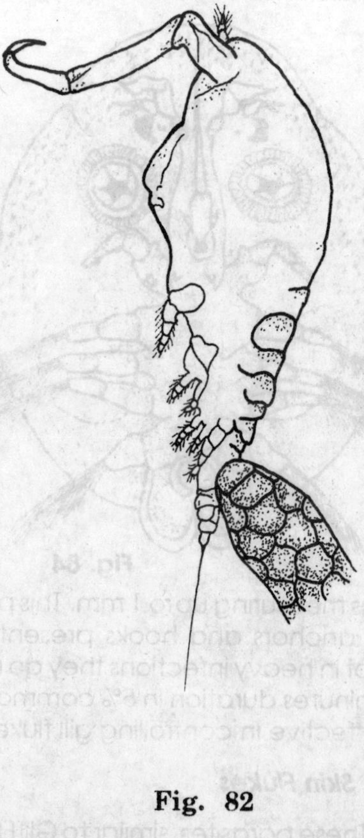

Fig. 82

parasites can be removed mechanically by means of forceps and the resulting wound can be cleaned by strong Potassium permanganate (5 ppm) or Mercurochrome solutions. Other copepod parasites like *Ergasilus* (Fig. 82) infest and damage the gills of tropical aquarium fishes.

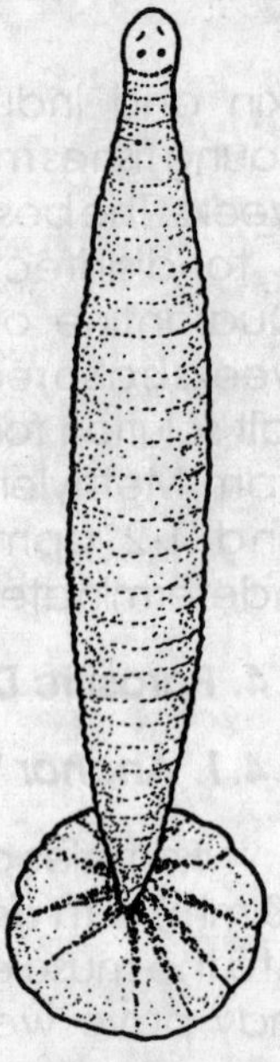

Fig. 83

6.4.2. Fish Leech (Fig. 83).

This worm-like animal with a large sucking disc at each end, grows to about 20 to 50 mm. They feed on the blood of fishes and thus cause emaciation and anaemia. The open bleeding wounds created by leeches become secondarily infected with bacteria and fungi. Moreover, they act as vectors for certain fish viruses and haemoflagellates. The best treatment for removing leech is to place the fish in 2 to 3% salt solution for 15 minutes.

6.4.3. Fish Lice (Argulus spp.) (Fig. 84).

Fish lice has a flattened disc-shaped body, 8 to 12 mm in diameter. The sucking type of mouth parts of this parasite are well adapted to pierce the host tissue and to suck the host's blood. Since these are large forms, they can be removed easily by means of forceps. *Argulus* can also be dislodged by a touch of strong salt solution with a brush. Heavy infection in culture ponds can be minimised by treating with Potassium permanganate (4 to 5 mg/l of water).

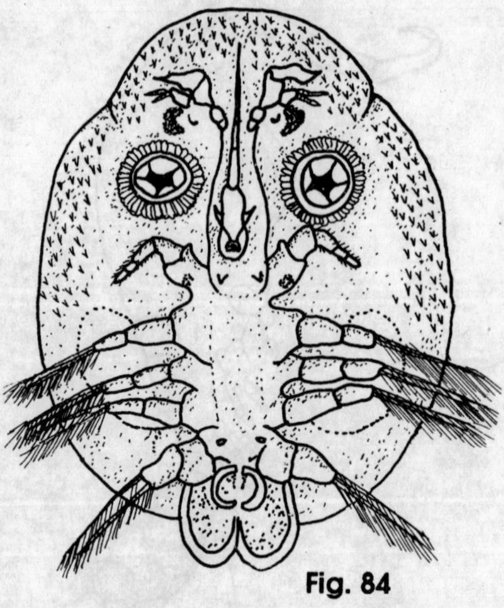

Fig. 84

6.4.4. Gill Flukes (Fig. 85).

Gill flukes in aquarium fishes are represented mainly by *Dactylogyrus* and related species. These are small flat worms measuring upto 1 mm. This parasite attaches itself to the gills of fishes using anchors and hooks present in the posterior part (Opisthohaptor). Except in heavy infections they do not produce much ill effects. Short baths of 5 minutes duration in 5% common salt or 5-10 minutes in 1 : 5000 formalin are effective in controlling gill flukes.

6.4.5. Skin Flukes

These parasites, similar to Gill Flukes, are represented in aquarium fishes mainly by the genus *Gyrodactylus.* Heavy infection results in copious

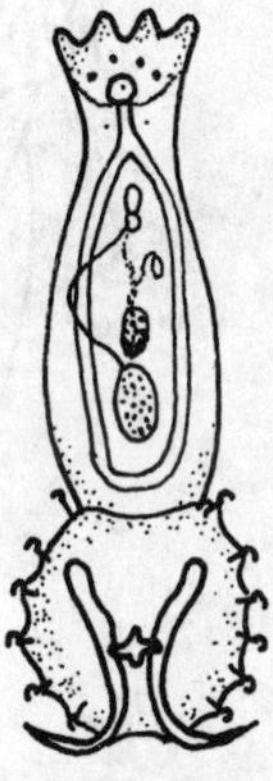

Fig. 85

mucous production and damage of the skin with accompanying scale loss. Heavily infected fish show abnormal swimming behaviour, rub their bodies against hard objects and try to jump out of water. It can be treated in the same way as that of gill flukes.

6.4.6. Intestinal Parasitic Worms

Generally, intestinal worms are not frequent in aquarium fishes. However, they are common in outdoor culture systems. They are represented mainly by Digeneans (sucking worms) (Fig. 86), Cestodes (tape worms) (Fig. 87), Acanthocephalans (spiny headed worms) (Fig. 88) and Nematodes (round worms) (Fig. 89). Except in heavy infections they do not produce much ill effects.

Fig. 86

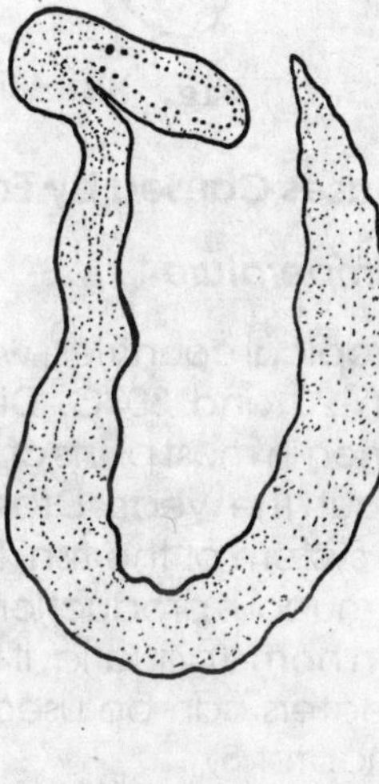

Fig. 87

Internal parasitic infections are difficult to control. Several antiparasitic drugs available in the market can be tried with varying level of success. Since the life histories of all these parasites include intermediate hosts like wild fish, annelids, crustaceans, snails,etc., it is very important to remove all these animals from aquaria and culture systems.

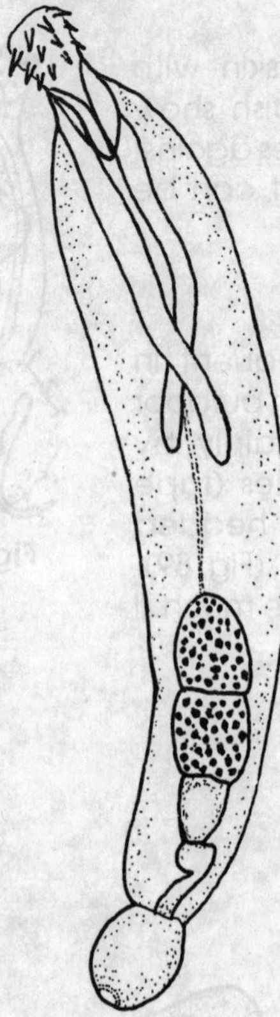

Fig. 88

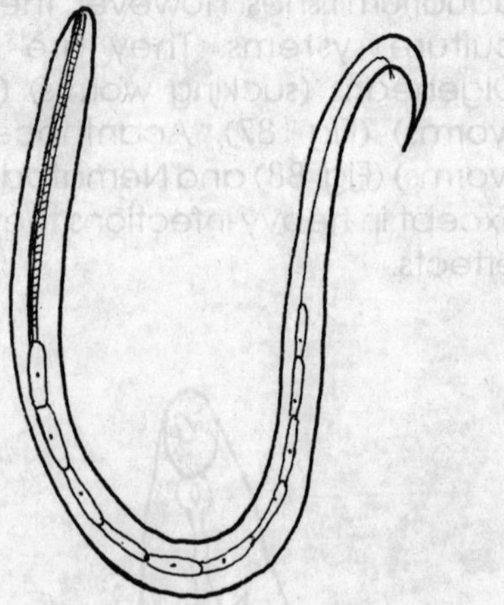

Fig. 89

6.5. Diseases Caused by Environmental Factors

6.5.1. Temperature

In tropical countries, water temperature is substantially higher, ranging between 20 and 30°C. Diseases due to temperature changes is rather uncommon in most parts of India since tempeature does not vary drastically throughout the year. Drastic temperature variations directly affect the immune system of the fish. Respiratory rate of fish is affected mainly due to copious mucous production; the gills turn white and in extreme cases, death follows. In home aquaria, if temperature comes down drastically i.e., below 15°C, heaters can be used to raise the temperature to the required level (refer chapter 3).

6.5.2. pH

Fishes withstand a pH range from 6 to 8 without much adverse effects. Carps cultured in water low pH (acidic) may develop a disease called acidaemia, characterised by brown colouration of gills, necrosis of epithelial cells, copious mucous production, etc. Alkaline water destroys the mucous layer which acts as the first level of defence mechanism in fishes.

6.5.3. Oxygen

Though the optimum oxygen requirement of tropical fishes is between 6 to 9 mg/L of water, some ornamental fishes with accessory respiratory organs like gouramies and catfishes survive at still lower oxygen concentrations. Absence or depletion of oxygen (anoxia or hypoxia) can occur during night or even in day time, under conditions of high temperature, low light and low atmospheric pressure, particularly in cloudy days. It can also be caused by algal blooms, overstocking and accumulation of waste materials.

Fish show signs of oxygen depletion in water by coming to the water surface, exhibiting rapid respiratory movements. Should this occur early in the night the addition of more fresh water or installation of aerating devices is advisable.

Supersaturation of the environment with oxygen cause the gas bubble disease or embolism. When the gas bubbles enter the blood vessels, they retard or stop the blood circulation. Affected fish may swim at 45° angle or tumble over. Death occurs due to embolism of gills and heart.

6.6. Nutritional Diseases

Since most of the people feed aquarium fishes with artificial food, care should be taken to provide a 'balanced diet'. Absence or reduction in the quantity of proteins, vitamins, etc. in fish food may lead to nutritional diseases. Both underfeeding and overfeeding are equally harmful to fishes. Inadequate quantity of food (underfeeding) results in starvation. Though this phenomenon is uncommon in aquaria and culture systems, some fishes refuse to take artificial food. Undernourished fish become weak and may easily fall prey to diseases and enemies.

Protein deficiency in food results in stunted growth, incomplete gonad development, loss of weight, cataract, skeletal deformities, etc. Presence of excess starch in the food may lead to liver malfunctioning. Deficiency of essential fatty acids in fish food leads to incomplete colouration, degeneration of fins, etc.

The deficiency of minerals and vitamins may also lead to diseases in fish. Even excess quantity of vitamins could be fatal. For example, excess of vitamin A in fish food leads to gill abnormalities, necrosis of fins, haemorrhages, etc.

6.7. Genetic Diseases

Normally genetic defects appear in less than 10% of the offsprings. The common genetic deformities are Lordosis (crooked back), abnormal morphology, etc. Since genetic diseases develop due to change in genetic material, treating such diseases is rather impossible. However, this can be reduced by adopting proper breeding techniques like cross breeding. Interestingly certain varieties of aquarium fishes like lion head and pop eyed goldfish are example of genetic abnormalities due to inbreeding.

6.8. Tumours

External tumours are visible as projecting lumps on the surface of the fish whereas internal tumours can be detected only when they distend the body. Tumours can be benign (simple) or malignant (cancerous). Tumours are represented in a wide variety of aquarium fishes like sword tails, mollies, cichlids, etc. Since most of the tumours are incurable, humane disposal of diseased fish is advisable.

6.9. Control of Diseases in Aquarium Fishes

You have seen in the above part that a wide variety of diseases occur in ornamental fishes. However, many of these diseases can be prevented or controlled upto a certain extent if you practise certain preventive or prophylactic measures. The dictum prevention is better than cure should be the objective in aquarium fish keeping and ornamental fish culture. The following preventive and prophylactic measures are recommended for successful fish keeping and culture.

1. To prevent the occurrence of diseases, aquarium should be disinfected with dilute Potassium permanganate solution before use. Ponds must be periodically dried and disinfected by liming.
2. Provide pathogen-free food and water.
3. Entry of unwanted animals and plants should be avoided since majority of these forms may carry pathogens or parasites into the aquarium.
4. Maintain optimum levels of temperature, light, pH and oxygen.
5. Before stocking it is advisable to stock the fishes in quarantine tanks and examine them for symptoms of diseases, if any. Infected fish should be disinfected before stocking.
6. The nets and other instruments used in aquarium should be periodically disinfected.
7. High stocking denisities and unnecessary handling of fishes should be avoided since these factors are responsible for 'stress' in fishes which may enhance the occurrence of diseases.

6.10. Common Diseases of Aquarium Fish: A Diagrammatic Representation

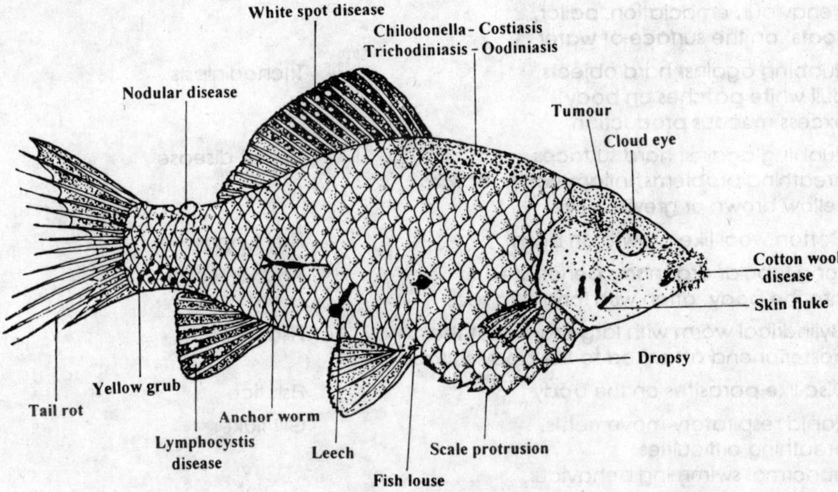

Fig. 90

6.11. Key for Identifying Comman Diseases

Symptoms	Disease
1. Abnormal swimming behaviour, pallor, cloudy eyes	Cloud eye/worm cataract
2. White threads or patches on head, frayed fin rays	Columnaris disease
3. Sunken or protruding eyes, swollen abdomen, scale protrusion	Dropsy
4. Disintegration of fin rays, starting from the tip and progressing towards the base, frayed fin rays.	Tail/Fin rot
5. Ulcerated body	Ulcer disease
6. Rubbing against hard objects, fast breathing movements, sloughing off of the skin.	Chilodonella
7. Rubbing against hard objects, closed fin, small white spots, on body and fins.	White spot disease
8. Erratic swimming, emaciation, white patches, disintegration of muscles	Neon Tetra disease
9. Small swellings and white spots on the body	Nodular disease

(Contd ...)

Symptoms	Disease
10. Listlessness, abnormal swimming behaviour, emaciation, pallor, floats' on the surface of water	Sleeping sickness
11. Rubbing against hard objects, dull white patches on body, excess mucous production	Trichodiniasis
12. Rubbing against hard surfaces, breathing problems, inflammation of skin, yellow brown or greyish haze.	Velvet disease
13. Cotton wool like growth on body	Fish fungus
14. Long tubular organisms penetrated into the body, often with long egg sacs.	Anchor worm
15. Cylindrical worm with large sucker at the posterior end attached to the body surface	Fish leech
16. Disc-like parasites on the body	Fish lice
17. Rapid respiratory movements, breathing difficulties, abnormal swimming behaviour, small worms on gills	Gill flukes
18. Emaciation, swollen abdomen, retarded growth	Intestinal parasites
19. Rubbing against hard objects, excess mucous production, inflammed patches on body, small worms on body surface	Skin flukes

GLOSSARY

Acclimatization : Individual adaptation of living things to changed conditions of life, especially to changes of climate.

Adipose fin : Small, fleshy fin found between the dorsal fin and the tail in some fishes like Piranhas.

Albino : Fish that lacks dark pigment and appears white or transparent; a hereditary disorder.

Anaemia : Condition in which the normal amount of red blood cells are reduced; paleness is the main symptom.

Anal fin : An unpaired fin between the anus and the tail, on underside of the fish.

Anoxia : Insufficient supply of oxygen.

Antibiotics : Drugs produced from molds or mold-like organisms, used either for inhibiting the growth of bacteria (bacteriostats) or for destroying the bacteria (bacteriocides).

Appetite : Desire for food.

Artemia : Generic name of brine shrimp, a small crustacean (arthropode) living in hypersaline water.

Barbel : Fleshy, beard-like part attached to the mouth of some fishes.

Brackish water : Water having salinity between that of seawater and freshwater.

Cancer : Cancer is a malignant tomour (see tumour). They choke out normal tissue as they extend to adjacent tissue layers by the rapid multiplication of cells

Cataract : Clouding of the lens of the eye.

Dropsy : Accumulation of fluids in the abdomen; oedema.

Emaciation : Excessive thinning of the body.

Embolism : Small clot, gas bubbles or foreign substances floating freely in blood stream. These substances (embolus) often obstruct blood circulation.

Exophthalmus (pop-eye) : Bulging of the eyes, mainly due to diseases.

Gonopodium : An anal fin that has been modified to form a copulatory organ in some male fishes. Eg. Guppy.

Haemorrhage : Severe loss of blood from a blood vessel.

Hormones : Secretions from endocrine (ductless) glands; having particular physiological function.

Host : Organism in which or on which a parasite lives.

Hybrid : A cross-bred product, coming from parents with different hereditary characteristics; generally hybrids are sterile. They show greater vigor and vitality.

Hybridization : The process of making a hybrid by mating two types of animals.

Hyperplasia : An abnormal increase in the number of normal cells.

Hypophysation : The process of inducing the fish for breeding, by injecting pituitary extract or sex hormones.

Hypoxia : A condition in which there is less than the normal content of oxygen in the organ and tissues.

Ichthyology : Study of fishes.

Inflammation : Changes that occur in living tissues when they are invaded by germs.

Intermediate host : The host organism in which the larval stage of the parasite develops before infecting the final host.

Lordosis : An abnormal curvature of the spine with the concavity towards the front.

Mucus : Slimy secretion by membranes to moisten and protect the skin.

Nauplius larva	:	A typical larva of Crustacea (Arthropoda) formed directly from the egg: a minute creature with rounded unsegmented body, 3 pairs of simple appendages and a median eye.
Necrosis	:	Death of a part of the body due to absence of blood supply.
Nodule	:	Small rounded protuberance; often formed by a group of cells or by the invasion of a parasite.
Nocturnal	:	Animals active during night time.
Operculum	:	The bony gill cover of fishes.
Pallor	:	Paleness of skin; a disease symptom.
Parasite	:	An organism which lives and feeds in or on another organism. Ectoparasites live on the surface of the host whereas endoparasites live inside the body of the host. In fish, gill parasites are usually referred to as ectoparasites.
Pathogen	:	Organism or anything capable of producing disease.
Pathology	:	Study of diseases.
Peat	:	An acid soil derived from decomposed plants, especially from moss.
Pectoral fins	:	The paired fins placed behind the gill openings of fishes.
Pelvic fins	:	The paired fins attached to the underside of fishes anterior to the anus.
pH	:	Concentration of hydrogen ions. The pH value of water shows whether the water is acid, neutral or alkaline. pH 7 is neutral; pH between 0 and 7 is acid and 7 and 14 is alkaline.
Photoperiodism	:	The reaction of any organism to the relative lengths of day and night.
Plankton	:	Small organisms occupying the top layers of water with feeble powers of locomotion; often transported with the help of winds.

ppm	:	Parts per million, a measure of concentration, The same as micrograms per millilitre or milligrams per litre.
Prophylaxis	:	Prevention of disease.
Quarantine tank	:	A tank in which diseased fishes are kept.
Rotifer	:	A tiny fresh or brackish water invertebrate with ciliated body. Important food for young fishes. Eg: *Brachionus*.
Spawning	:	The deposition of eggs by aquatic animals.
Species	:	A basic taxonomic unit of animals and plants. Members of a species resemble each other and interbreed but do not normally interbreed with other species.
Standard length	:	In fish, length is often measured as standard length; it is the distance from the tip of the snout to the caudal peduncle, behind the origin of the caudal fin.
Tranquilizer	:	Calming agent.
Tubifex worms	:	A group of small freshwater segmented worms that live on mud and other decaying organic matter.
Tumour	:	A true tumour is a part of a tissue with excessive growth due to cell division, out of the control of the host organism. Tumour may be 'benign' or 'malignant'. A benign tumour grows slowly and is restricted to its original site. Malignant tumours grow invasively and rapidly. Malignant tumours are otherwise called cancers or sarcomas.
Ulcer	:	Sores on skin or internal parts formed by various things.
Vector	:	An animal which carries parasites or pathogenic organisms to the host.
Ventral fins	:	Paired fins on the underside of a fish in front of the anus.